ALDEN'S

CITIZEN'S MANUAL.

A TEXT-BOOK ON GOVERNMENT,

FOR

COMMON SCHOOLS.

BY

REV. JOSEPH ALDEN, D.D., LL.D.,

PRESIDENT OF THE STATE NORMAL SCHOOL, ALBANY, N.Y., AUTHOR OF "ELEMENTS OF INTELLECTUAL PHILOSOPHY," "THE SCIENCE OF GOVERNMENT," "CHRISTIAN ETHICS," ETC.

NEW YORK:
SHELDON AND COMPANY.
1869.

DR. ALDEN'S BOOKS ON GOVERNMENT

ARE

THE YOUNG CITIZEN'S MANUAL:
A Text-Book for Common Schools. One volume, 12mo, half bd. Price 50 cts.

THE SCIENCE OF GOVERNMENT
IN CONNECTION WITH AMERICAN INSTITUTIONS. A Text-Book for High Schools, Academies, and Colleges. One volume, 12mo. Price $1.50.

STEREOTYPED AT THE
BOSTON STEREOTYPE FOUNDRY,
No. 4 Spring Lane.

PREFACE.

The publishers of the "Science of Government in connection with American Institutions," — a work designed for Colleges and High Schools, — have received abundant assurances, from various parts of the country, that the general introduction of the study of the science of government into common schools would follow the appearance of a text-book adapted to the wants and circumstances of common school teachers. The author was thus led to consult a number of intelligent and experienced teachers. Having possessed himself of their views, which met his full approbation, he prepared a work, and submitted it to an able and successful teacher, who carefully revised every part of it, and made many valuable suggestions. The work was then wholly re-written, and is now given to the public with the hope that it will meet the approbation of common school teachers, and aid them in doing a work which no other class of men can do — that of preparing the masses for intelligently exercising their rights as citizens of the Republic.

The teacher who may use this little volume will find its topics more fully treated in the "Science of Government," above mentioned.

J. A.

Pond.

CONTENTS.

THE

YOUNG CITIZEN'S MANUAL.

CHAPTER I.

ORIGIN OF CIVIL SOCIETY AND GOVERNMENT.

1. *Why do men live together in society?*

Because God made them to live together in society.

2. *How does that appear?*

God has given to men a social nature, which renders society necessary to their happiness and improvement.

3. *If a man is willing to forego the advantages of society, may he not cease to be a member of it?*

He has no right to forego the advantages of society.

4. *How does that appear?*

God designed that he should live in society and enjoy its benefits, and he has no right to act contrary to that design.

5. *What is necessary in order that men may live together in peace in society?*

There must be good laws obeyed and enforced.

6. *Why are laws necessary?*

They are necessary to restrain men from interfering with one another's rights.

7. *How does this appear?*

Experience has shown that some men are disposed to act unjustly, and hence need to be restrained by law.

8. *Who makes and executes the laws?*

The government.

9. *Who make the government?*

The people.

10. *May the people make just such a government as they choose?*

They may, provided it is adapted to secure justice and the public prosperity.

11. *What power does the government possess?*

The power conferred upon it by the people.

12. *Can the people authorize the government to act unjustly?*

They cannot. Justice is the fundamental law which both the people and the government are under obligation to obey.

13. *What is the instrument by which the people determine the form and define the powers of government?*

The Constitution.

14. *Who make the laws?*

The legislature.

15. *What is the legislature?*

A body of men chosen by the people to make laws.

16. *What is the difference between the Constitution and the laws made by the legislature?*

The Constitution is the higher law, to which all the laws enacted by the legislature must be conformed.

17. *Is there any higher law than the Constitution?*

The Constitution is the highest human law; but the law of God is the highest of all laws.

18. *May not the people who make the Constitution disobey it if they please?*

The people, as well as the government, are under obligation to obey the Constitution.

19. *May the people change the Constitution?*

They may change it in the way pointed out by the Constitution.

20. *How does it appear that it is God's will that the people should have government?*

It appears from the fact that government is necessary to the existence of society and the well-being of men, and from the Bible.

21. *What does the Bible say on the subject?*

"The powers that be are ordained of God;" which is the same as saying, "Government is ordained of God."

22. *What does the Bible say respecting magistrates?*

It commands us "to obey magistrates."

23. *Suppose their commands come in conflict with the law of God?*

Then "we ought to obey God rather than men."—Acts 5:29.

24. *Is it ever right to resist the government?*
It is sometimes right to resort to revolution.

25. *What is meant by the right of revolution?*
The right to overthrow the government by force, and establish another in its place.

26. *When may the right of revolution be resorted to?*
When the oppression is very great, and the prospect of success good.

CHAPTER II.

MONARCHY. — ARISTOCRACY. — REPUBLIC. — LIBERTY AND LAW.

1. *Who determine the form of the government?*
The people.

2. *What are the three forms of government?*
Monarchy, aristocracy, and republic.

3. *What is a monarchy?*
A monarchy is a government by a single person.*

4. *What is an absolute monarchy?*
One in which all the powers of the government are possessed by the monarch.

5. *What is a limited monarchy?*
One in which the power of the monarch is limited by the Constitution and laws.

---

* "The titles of the different monarchs of Europe are, *Emperor*, *Czar*, or *Sultan*, the ruler of an empire; *King* or *Queen*, of a kingdom; *Prince*, of a principality; *Grand Duke*, of a grand duchy; *Duke*, of a duchy; and *Pope*, of the popedom." — *Worcester*.

6. *What is an hereditary monarchy?*

One in which the oldest surviving son or nearest heir succeeds to the crown on the death of the monarch.

7. *What is an elective monarchy?*

One in which the monarch is elected by the people, or by some portion of them.

8. *What is an aristocracy?*

Aristocracy "is a form of government which places the supreme power in the nobles, or the principal persons of the state."

9. *What may be said of this form of government?*

It is the worst form.

10. *What is a republic?*

A republic is that form of government in which the power of the state is exercised by agents chosen by the people.

11. *What is a democracy?*

Democracy is a government by the people.

12. *What is a pure democracy?*

One in which the power of the state is exercised directly by the people.

13. *What is a representative democracy?*

A representative democracy does not differ from a republic.

14. *Are the three forms of government — monarchy, aristocracy, and republic — always kept separate?*

They are not. The three forms are blended in the English government.

15. *What is the best form of government?*

That which is the best adapted to promote justice and the public prosperity.

16. *What should determine the form of a nation's government?*

The character and circumstances of the people.

17. *For what nations is a republic the best form?*

Those in which the people are intelligent and moral.

18. *Why are representatives chosen?*

Because all the people of a nation cannot meet together, and make laws.

19. *For what other reason?*

Because men selected on account of their wisdom are best qualified to make laws.

20. *To whom are the representatives responsible?*

To the people and to God.

21. *Do wise and just laws interfere with liberty?*

They do not. Civil liberty is the result of law.

22. *What can men reasonably claim?*

Liberty to do right, and protection against wrong.

23. *Do laws which restrain a man from doing wrong infringe on his liberty?*

They do not; for he has no right to do wrong.

24. *What would perfectly wise laws require?*

They would require men to do what is just.

25. *What would they prohibit?*

Everything unjust.

26. *What would be the result of perfectly wise laws faithfully executed?*

Every one would be at liberty to do right, and would be secure from wrong.

27. *If one was free to do right, and secure against wrong, what would he have?*

Perfect liberty.

28. *What, then, is the relation between liberty and law?*

The perfection of law would secure the perfection of liberty.

CHAPTER III.

DESPOTISM. — FREE GOVERNMENT. — RIGHT AND DUTY OF SELF-GOVERNMENT.

1. *What is a despotic government?*

A government in which the rulers exercise irresponsible power.

2. *May a republican government be despotic?*

Those intrusted with power by the people may, for a time, use that power in a despotic manner.

3. *What is the remedy in such a case?*

The remedy is found in the ballot-box. Other men must be elected to wield the powers of government.

4. *What is a military despotism?*

Government by a military despot whose will is the sole law.

5. *What is a free government?*

A government of laws securing liberty.

6. *May not an absolute despot make wise and just laws?*

He may.

7. *Would not such laws secure liberty?*

They would for the time being; but there would be no security for their continuance.

8. *Why would there be no security?*

Because they would depend upon the will of one man, whose will might change at any moment.

9. *Is government by the people necessarily a free government?*

Not necessarily; for the people, or a majority of them, may construct a government which will not secure liberty.

10. *Have the people a right to govern themselves?*

It is both their right and duty to govern themselves wisely and righteously.

11. *How have governments often originated?*

In fraud and force, and not in the consent of the people governed.

12. *May such governments become legitimate?*

They may.

13. *How may they become legitimate?*

Only by becoming good governments, and receiving either the express or the tacit consent of the people.

14. *What do you mean by a legitimate government?*

A lawful government.

15. *May it be the duty of a people to obey a military despot?*

It may be the duty of a people to obey a despot for a time.

16. *How does that appear?*

Christ taught the duty of obedience to Cæsar, who was a military despot.

17. *On what ground may it be our duty to obey a military despot?*

On the ground that any government is better than anarchy, or lawlessness.

18. *How long may it be the duty of a people to obey a military despot?*

Till they can overthrow his government, and establish a better one in its place.

19. *What is meant by the divine right of kings?*

The claim put forth by some monarchs that they received their power directly from God, and not from the people.

20. *What doctrine was founded upon this claim?*

The doctrine of passive obedience and non-resistance.

21. *What did that doctrine teach?*

It taught that implicit, unquestioning obedience should be given to the government, and that no resistance should be made even to the most oppressive acts.

22. *Are the people infallible in matters of government?*

No individual is infallible; hence no collection of individuals is infallible.

23. *Can an ignorant and vicious people establish and maintain a free government?*

Reason and experience show that they cannot.

24. *What are the greatest safeguards of freedom?*

Intelligence and morality on the part of the people.

CHAPTER IV.

COLONIAL GOVERNMENTS.

1. *When did the Pilgrims land at Plymouth?*

December 22, 1620.

2. *In what ship did they cross the ocean?*

The May Flower.

3. *Before leaving the May Flower, what provision did they make for government?*

They drew up and signed a compact binding themselves to obey the laws which should be made by the majority.

4. *What officers did they choose?*

A governor and an assistant.

5. *Who made the laws?*

The people of the colony.

6. *How long did this state of things continue?*

Until 1639 — nineteen years.

7. *What change then took place?*

The settlements had become so widely extended that it was inconvenient for the people to assemble and make laws.

8. *What measures were then taken?*

The people elected representatives to meet and make laws for them.

9. *Did the representatives thus elected constitute the first legislative assembly in America?*

No; the first representative legislature sat in Virginia in 1619.*

10. *In what respect were the governments of all the colonies similar?*

Each colony had a governor, a council constituting the upper house of the legislature, and representatives chosen by the people, constituting the lower house.

---

* Previous to 1619, the people of Virginia had been governed by a governor and council appointed by the king of Great Britain. The people then claimed the right, as British subjects, to be represented in the government. Sir George Yeardley, the governor, permitted the various plantations to elect representatives, who formed the lower house of the legislature, the council forming the upper house.

11. *How were the governors appointed?*

In most of the colonies, they were appointed by the king.

12. *What powers had the colonial legislatures?*

They had power to make laws for their respective colonies, provided the laws made were not contrary to the laws of Great Britain.

13. *What power had the governors?*

They had power to veto any and every act of the legislatures; that is, to prevent the act from becoming a law.

14. *What powers had the governor and council acting together?*

They had power to establish courts and appoint judges, to raise troops and proclaim martial law in cases of invasion or rebellion.

15. *Had the colonists much liberty?*

They had the forms of liberty, without the substance.

16. *Who possessed the political power?*

All real power was possessed by the king, or by those holding office at his will.

17. *Were the colonies united under one general government?*

They were united only in a common relation to the crown and to the mother country.

18. *On what ground did the colonists claim that they should not be taxed without their consent?*

On the ground that they were entitled to all the privileges of Englishmen, especially that of representation.

19. *What led to the revolution?*

The attempt of the Parliament of Great Britain to raise a revenue in the colonies while denying them representation in Parliament.

2

20. *What act of Parliament was passed for that purpose?*

The Stamp Act, which required the colonists to use stamped paper for all legal documents.

21. *What state took the lead in opposition to the measures of the British government?*

Massachusetts recommended that a Congress of deputies from all the colonies should assemble to deliberate on the state of affairs.

22. *When and where did this Congress meet?*

In Philadelphia, September 4, 1774.

23. *How were the delegates to this Congress appointed?*

In some colonies by the lower branches of the legislatures, and in others by conventions of the people held for that purpose.

24. *When and where did the second Congress meet?*

In May, 1775, in Philadelphia.

25. *What were some of the acts of this Congress?*

They appointed George Washington commander-in-chief of the troops of the colonies, and declared independence July 4, 1776.

CHAPTER V.

THE CONFEDERATION.

1. *When did Congress appoint a committee to prepare Articles of Union between the states?*

On the 11th of June, 1776, the same day on which they appointed a committee to prepare the Declaration of Independence.

2. *What were the Articles thus prepared by Congress called?*

Articles of Confederation and of Perpetual Union between the States.

3. *When were they adopted by Congress?*

November, 1777.

4. *When were the Articles to become binding on the states?*

When adopted by the legislatures of all the states.

5. *When did they become binding?*

In March, 1781, nearly five years after the declaration of independence.

6. *Were the states separate, independent states up to that time?*

They were; but Congress had by general consent assumed the powers of a government for the United States.

7. *What has that government been called?*

The revolutionary government.

8. *What was the government established by the "Articles" called?*

The government of the Confederation.

9. *Where were the powers of this government vested?*

In Congress.

10. *Of how many Houses did Congress consist?*

It consisted of one House.

11. *How were the members appointed?*

By the legislatures of the states.

12. *How many delegates could each state send?*

No state could send less than two nor more than seven.

13. *For what length of time were the delegates appointed?*

For one year; but each state could recall its delegates at any time, and send others in their stead.

14. *How was the voting done in Congress?*

Each state had one vote, which was determined by a majority of its delegates.

15. *What were some of the powers of Congress?*

Congress had power to declare war and make peace; to coin money; to regulate the standard of weights and measures; to establish post-offices; to borrow money on the credit of the United States, and to emit bills of credit; to ascertain the amount of money needed by the United States, and to apportion the same among the states; to agree upon the number of the land forces, and apportion them among the states; to build and equip a navy; and to appoint one of their number to preside in Congress.

16. *What was the presiding officer called?*

The President of Congress.

17. *Was there any President of the United States with powers similar to those the President now has?*

No.

18. *Had Congress power to lay and collect taxes?*

It had not.

19. *Had Congress power to regulate commerce with foreign nations?*

It had not.

20. *How were all important matters determined?*

By the consent of nine states.

21. *How many states were there at that time?*

Thirteen.

22. *Had Congress power to establish a national judiciary?*

It had not.

23. *What courts could it establish?*

Courts for "receiving and determining finally appeals in all cases of captures."

24. *What was the great defect of the government of the Confederation?*

Its want of power.*

25. *Towards what were things tending?*

Towards a state which threatened to place the people in a worse condition than they were in before the revolution.†

CHAPTER VI.

FORMATION AND ADOPTION OF THE CONSTITUTION.

1. *What measures were taken to remedy the defects of the Confederation?*

A Convention was called for that purpose.

2. *Who recommended the calling of a Convention?*

Congress.

---

* "The Confederation," said Washington, "seems to me to be little more than a shadow without the substance, and Congress a nugatory body, their ordinances being little attended to."

† Washington, in view of the state of things, wrote that it might be "a subject of regret that so much blood and treasure have been lavished to no purpose, that so many sufferings have been encountered without compensation, and that so many sacrifices have been made in vain."

3. *Who were especially influential in bringing about that event?*

James Madison and Alexander Hamilton.

4. *How were the delegates to the Convention appointed?*

By the legislatures of the states.

5. *Did all the states send delegates?*

All except Rhode Island.

6. *What was the Convention called?*

The Federal Convention.

7. *Where and when did it meet?*

In Philadelphia, May 5, 1787.

8. *Who was chosen President of the Convention?*

George Washington.

9. *What was one of the rules of the Convention?*

That the proceedings of the Convention should be kept secret.

10. *How did those proceedings become known?*

Mr. Madison made a daily record of them, and after his death that record was published by order of Congress.

11. *What was the Convention expected to do?*

To revise and amend the Articles of Confederation.

12. *Of what was a majority of the Convention soon convinced?*

That something more than a revision and amendment of the Articles was needed.

13. *What was the first resolution adopted by the Convention?*

"Resolved, that a national government ought to be established, with a supreme legislative, executive, and judiciary."

14. *Were all the members of the Convention in favor of that resolution?*

There were some who insisted that they were appointed to amend the Articles of Confederation, and that they had no right to proceed to form a national government.

15. *Was the question of abandoning the Confederation, or league of the states, and of forming a national government for the United States, brought distinctly before the Convention?*

It was.

16. *How did the states, by their delegates, vote on that question?*

Massachusetts, Connecticut, Pennsylvania, Virginia, North Carolina, South Carolina, and Georgia — seven states — voted for the national plan.

17. *What states voted for the league plan?*

New York, New Jersey, and Delaware — three states. The vote of Maryland was divided.

18. *What did the Convention then proceed to do?*

To form the Constitution.

19. *Was the formation of the Constitution a difficult work?*

It was a work of so great difficulty that Washington wrote to a friend, "I almost despair of seeing a favorable issue to the proceedings of the Convention, and I do therefore regret that I have had any agency in the business."

20. *What was done with the Constitution when finished by the Convention?*

It was published and laid before Conventions called by the legislatures of the states to adopt or to reject it.

21. *Who were prominent among the writers in favor of the Constitution?*

Alexander Hamilton, James Madison, and John Jay.

22. *What is the work written by them called?*

The Federalist.

23. *What were the friends of the Constitution called?*

Federalists.

24. *What were its opponents called?*

Anti-Federalists.

25. *How was the Constitution adopted?*

By state conventions.

26. *What states adopted the Constitution unanimously?*

Delaware, New Jersey, and Georgia.

27. *What states adopted it by large majorities?*

Pennsylvania, Maryland, and South Carolina.

28. *What states adopted it by small majorities?*

Massachusetts, New York, and Virginia.

29. *What state rejected it?*

North Carolina.

30. *What state did not call a Convention to consider it?*

Rhode Island.

31. *How many states were required to ratify the Constitution before it could go into operation?*

Nine states.

32. *What was done by Congress when eleven states had ratified it?*

On the 13th of September, 1788, Congress appointed the first Wednesday of January, 1789, for the choice of electors for President, and the first Wednesday of March following for commencing proceedings under the new Constitution.

33. *Who were elected President and Vice-President?*

George Washington and John Adams.

34. *When and where did the first Congress under the Constitution meet?*

On the 4th of March, 1789, in New York.

35. *When were the votes for President counted?*

On the 6th of April.

36. *Why were they not counted sooner?*

Because a quorum of both houses of Congress did not assemble till that time.

37. *When was Washington sworn into office?*

On the 30th of April, 1789.

38. *Who were members of his Cabinet?*

Thomas Jefferson was Secretary of State, Alexander Hamilton, Secretary of the Treasury, Henry Knox, Secretary of War, and Edmund Randolph, Attorney-General.

39. *Did the Constitution go into full operation when Washington was sworn into office?*

It did not, because Congress had first to pass organizing the different departments.

40. *Did all the officers of the Confederation cease to act on the 4th of March,* 1789?

They did not, but continued to attend to their departments until relieved by officers appointed under the Constitution.

41. *When was the Constitution in full operation?*

In the autumn of 1789.

42. *When did North Carolina and Rhode Island adopt the Constitution?*

North Carolina adopted it in November, 1789, and Rhode Island in May, 1790.

QUESTIONS FOR REVIEW.

ORIGIN OF SOCIETY AND GOVERNMENT.

1. Is society of human or divine origin?
2. What is meant when it is said that society is of divine origin?
3. Are men under obligation to live in society?
4. Why are laws necessary?
5. Who make and execute the laws?
6. How does it appear that it is God's will that there should be government?
7. What is the fundamental law of society and government?
8. What are the three forms of government?
9. Who determine the form of government?
10. What is the best form of government?
11. For what nations is a republic the best form?
12. On what ground may it be the duty of a people to obey a despotic government?
13. In what way may a government established by fraud or force become a lawful government?
14. When did the Pilgrims land at Plymouth?
15. By whom were their laws made at first?
16. How were they made when the population became more numerous?
17. Is convenience the only reason for choosing representatives?
18. What other reason can be given?
19. When and where did the first legislative assembly meet in America?

20. In what respects were the Colonial governments similar?
21. What powers had the Colonial legislatures?
22. By whom was all real power retained?
23. What led to the Revolution?
24. What state recommended a meeting of delegates from the Colonies?
25. When and where did the first Congress meet?
26. When did the second Congress meet?
27. What was the distinguishing act of that Congress?
28. What measures did it take to unite the states?
29. When were the Articles of Confederation adopted by all the states?
30. Where were the powers of the Confederation vested?
31. Of how many houses did Congress consist?
32. How was the voting done?
33. What was the great defect of the Confederation?
34. Could it lay and collect taxes and raise soldiers?
35. What could it do when money and men were wanted?
36. Who took the lead in measures for forming the Constitution?
37. When and where did the Federal Convention meet?
38. With what purpose did a majority of the members come together?
39. What was the first resolution passed by the Convention?
40. What did they then proceed to do?
41. Was the formation of the Constitution a work of difficulty?
42. How was the Constitution adopted?
43. How many states had adopted it when it went into operation?
44. When were the electors for President chosen?
45. Who was the first President?
46. When and where did the first Congress under the Constitution meet?

CHAPTER VII.

THE NATURE OF THE CONSTITUTION.

1. *How is the Constitution divided as to its form?*

It is divided into articles, sections, and paragraphs.

2. *How many articles did the Constitution contain when it was adopted?*

Seven.

3. *How many have since been added as amendments?*

Thirteen.

4. *Are these amendments as much a part of the Constitution as the original articles?*

They are.

5. *Repeat the Preamble of the Constitution?*

"We, the people of the United States, in order to form a more perfect union, establish justice, insure domestic tranquillity, provide for the common defence, and promote the general welfare, and secure the blessings of liberty to ourselves and our posterity, do ordain and establish this Constitution for the United States of America."

6. *By whom was the Constitution ordained and established?*

By the people of the United States.

7. *By whom then can the Constitution be altered or abolished?*

By the people of the United States.*

---

* An early decision of the Supreme Court declares, "The Constitution of the United States was ordained and established not by the states in their sovereign capacity, but emphatically as *the Constitution* declares, by 'the people of the United States.'"

8. *When is an act said to be performed by the people of the United States?*

When it is performed by a majority of the people.

9. *Is the Constitution a league between the States?*

No; it is the fundamental law of a national government for the people of the United States.

10. *Why may not a state withdraw or secede from the Union?*

Because the Constitution does not authorize it.

11. *Suppose Congress should make a law contrary to the Constitution, may not the people of a state declare it null and void?*

They have no right or power to do so.

12. *What would be the remedy in case Congress should pass such a law?*

The Supreme Court would declare it null and void.

13. *By what authority would it do so?*

By authority given it by the Constitution.

14. *How does that appear?*

It appears from the express language of the Constitution.

15. *Quote the language in point.*

"This Constitution . . . shall be the supreme law of the land, and the judges in every state shall be bound thereby, anything in the Constitution and laws of any state to the contrary notwithstanding."

16. *How does it appear that the Supreme Court has power to declare laws that are contrary to the Constitution null and void?*

The Constitution says, "The judicial power shall extend to all cases in law or equity arising under this Constitution, the laws of the United States," &c.

17. *Does the Supreme Court decide upon the constitutionality of the laws before they go into operation?*

It does not.

18. *Can any one who deems a law unconstitutional refer it to the Supreme Court for a decision?*

He cannot. In order that the court may pronounce a decision on a law, it must be legally brought before the court in a case to be adjudicated.

19. *Is the decision of the Supreme Court final?*

It is.

20. *Suppose it should be erroneous?*

There is no help for it. It must stand till reversed by the same court, or by an amendment to the Constitution.

21. *Can the states be properly termed sovereign states?*

They cannot, for they have not sovereign power.

22. *What is sovereign power?*

Sovereign power is supreme power; the Constitution is the supreme law of the land.

CHAPTER VIII.

DIVISION OF POWERS. — CONGRESS. — HOUSE OF REPRESENTATIVES.

1. *How are the powers of government divided by the Constitution?*

They are divided into three departments, viz., the legislative, the judicial, and the executive.

2. *What is the office of the legislative department?*

To make the laws.

3. *What is the office of the judicial department?*

To interpret and apply the laws.

4. *What is the office of the executive department?*

To execute the laws.

5. *Why should not one man or one set of men make, interpret, and execute the laws?*

Experience has shown that there is greater security for justice when the three departments of government are separate.

6. *Should the different departments be independent of one another?*

They should be as far as is practicable.

7. *Suppose the judges were dependent on the executive for their offices and salaries?*

They might be tempted to consult his wishes rather than the dictates of justice.

8. *Is it practicable to make the different departments of government entirely independent of one another?*

It is not.

9. *What constitutes the legislative department of the government of the United States?*

Congress.

10. *Repeat Art.* I. *Sec.* 1 *of the Constitution.*

"All legislative powers herein granted shall be vested in a Congress of the United States, which shall consist of a Senate and House of Representatives."

11. *Why should Congress consist of two houses instead of one?*

Two houses furnish greater security for wise legislation; for if a bill passes one house without due consideration, its defects may be discovered in the other house.

12. *How is the House of Representatives composed?*

"The House of Representatives shall be composed of members chosen every second year by the people of the several states, and the electors in each state shall have the qualifications requisite for electors of the most numerous branch of the state legislature." — Art. I. § 2. 1.

13. *Why should not the representatives be elected for one year instead of two?*

If chosen for one year only, the members would scarcely become familiar with their duties and the mode of doing business before their term of service would expire.

14. *Why, then, was not a longer term than two years fixed upon?*

The term, as it now stands, was the result of compromise between those who preferred to have the representatives elected annually and those who preferred to have them elected for a longer period.

15. *What qualifications are required for a representative?*

"No person shall be a representative who shall not have attained to the age of twenty-five years, and been seven years a citizen of the United States, and who shall not, when elected, be an inhabitant of that state in which he shall be chosen." — Art. I. § 2. 2.

16. *To whom is reference made in the expression, "seven years a citizen of the United States"?*

To foreigners.

17. *How do foreigners become citizens?*

By becoming naturalized according to law.

18. *Why must a foreigner be a citizen for seven years before he can be a representative?*

To give him time to become weaned from his native land, and to become more strongly attached to the land of his adoption.

19. *Could a citizen of Boston be elected a representative from New York?*

He could not; because the Constitution requires the representative to be an inhabitant of the state for which he is chosen.

20. *What are congressional districts?*

Each state is by a law of the state divided into as many congressional districts as it has representatives.

21. *Does the Constitution require that such a division be made?*

It does not.

22. *Must the representative be an inhabitant of the district for which he is chosen?*

The Constitution does not require it, but it is the established custom.

23. *How are representatives apportioned among the states?*

"Representatives and direct taxes shall be apportioned among the several states which may be included within this Union, according to their respective numbers, which shall be determined by adding to the whole number of free persons, including those bound to service for a term of years, and excluding Indians not taxed, three fifths of all other persons." — Art. I. § 2. 3.

24. *What is meant by "three fifths of all other persons"?*

Slaves.

25. *How is the number of the people known?*

The Constitution requires that the census shall be taken, that is, that the people shall be numbered, every ten years.

26. *What is the constitutional provision as to the number of representatives?*

"The number of representatives shall not exceed one for every thirty thousand; but each state shall have at least one representative." — Art. I. § 2. 3.

27. *As the population has increased, has the ratio of representatives been enlarged?*

Congress has from time to time enlarged the ratio to prevent the house from having too many members.

28. *What is the present ratio?*

One representative for one hundred and twenty-seven thousand inhabitants.

29. *Do the representatives vote by states or by individuals?*

Each member has one vote.

30. *Suppose a representative should die or resign?*

"When vacancies happen in the representation from any state, the executive authority thereof shall issue writs of election to fill such vacancies." — Art. I. § 2. 4.)

31. *What is meant by the executive of a state?*

The governor.

32. *Who is the presiding officer of the House of Representatives?*

"The House of Representatives shall choose their Speaker and other officers, and shall have the sole power of impeachment." — Art. I. § 2. 5.)

33. *What is impeachment?*

A formal written accusation of an officer under government as guilty of some public offence or misdemeanor.

CHAPTER IX.

THE SENATE.

1. *How is the Senate composed?*

"The Senate of the United States shall be composed of two senators from each state, chosen by the legislature thereof, for six years; and each senator shall have one vote." — Art. I. § 3.

2. *Why are senators chosen for a longer period than representatives?*

Because they have duties to perform which are thought to require greater experience.

3. *What are some of those duties?*

They share with the President the responsibility of appointing men to office, and are connected with him in managing the foreign affairs of the government.

4. *How did the Constitution, at first, require the Senate to be divided?*

"Immediately after they shall be assembled in consequence of the first election, they shall be divided as equally as may be into three classes. The seats of the senators of the first class shall be vacated at the expiration of the second year; of the second class, at the expiration of the fourth year; and of the third class, at the expiration of the sixth year; so that one third may be chosen every second year." — Art. I. § 3. 2.

5. *What was the design of this provision?*

The main design was to make the changes in the Senate gradual.

6. *Do some senators now serve only two years, or do all serve six years.*

All senators now serve for six years, except those who may be chosen to fill the places of those whose term of service may not have expired.

7. *What are the qualifications for a senator?*

"No person shall be a senator who shall not have attained to the age of thirty years, and been nine years a citizen of the United States, and who shall not, when elected, be an inhabitant of that state for which he shall be chosen." — Art. I. § 3. 3.

8. *Have the small states as much power in the Senate as the large states?*

They have, because each has two senators, and thus two votes.*

9. *Who is the presiding officer of the Senate?*

"The Vice-President of the United States shall be President of the Senate, but shall have no vote unless they be equally divided." — Art. I. § 3. 4.

10. *Why should not the Senate choose one of their own number to preside?*

It would interfere with the equality of the states in the Senate.

11. *What is done when the Vice-President is absent?*

"The Senate shall choose their other officers, and also a president *pro tempore* in the absence of the vice-president, or when he shall exercise the office of President of the United States." — Art. I. § 3. 5.

---

* This provision was the result of compromise. Under the Confederation, the states had equal power, each state having one vote in Congress. When the Constitution was formed, the small states yielded their equality in the House, and retained it in the Senate.

12. *What is the custom of the Senate in regard to the choice of a president pro tempore?*

The Vice-President vacates the senatorial chair a short time before the end of each session, in order that the Senate may choose a president *pro tempore*, who is thus already in office if the Vice-President is called, in the recess, to exercise the office of President.

13. *Suppose a senator should die or resign?*

"If vacancies happen by resignation or otherwise, during the recess of the legislature of any state, the executive thereof may make temporary appointments until the next meeting of the legislature, which shall then fill such vacancies." — Art. I. § 3. 2.

14. *What judicial power does the Senate possess?*

"The Senate shall have the sole power to try all impeachments. When sitting for that purpose, they shall be on oath or affirmation." — Art. I. § 3. 6.

15. *Where is the power of impeachment vested?*

In the House of Representatives.

16. *Suppose the President of the United States should be impeached and tried?*

"When the President of the United States is tried, the Chief-Justice shall preside; and no person shall be convicted without the concurrence of two thirds of the members present." — Art. I. § 3. 6.

17. *Why should not the Vice-President preside when the President is tried?*

Because he would succeed to the office of President in case the President were convicted and removed from office.

18. *Why is a vote of two thirds required to convict a man?*

It is an additional security against injustice.

19. *Suppose the impeached person is found guilty, what punishment can be inflicted?*

"Judgment in cases of impeachment shall not extend further than to removal from office, and disqualification to hold and enjoy any office of honor, trust, or profit under the United States; but the party convicted shall nevertheless be liable and subject to indictment, trial, judgment, and punishment according to law." — Art. I. § 3. 7.

20. *Suppose the President of the United States, or some other civil officer, should be impeached for treason or murder, and convicted, could he be punished by death?*

Not by the Senate: the Senate could only remove him from office, and disfranchise him. He could then be tried by a court of law, and punished like any other criminal.

CHAPTER X.

MEETINGS OF CONGRESS.—PRIVILEGES OF MEMBERS.

1. *Who determine the times, places, and manner of holding elections for senators and representatives?*

"The times, places, and manner of holding elections for senators and representatives shall be prescribed in each state by the legislature thereof; but Congress may at any time, by law, make or alter such regulations, except as to the place of choosing senators." — Art. I. § 4. 1.

2. *How often must Congress assemble?*

"The Congress shall assemble at least once in every year, and such meeting shall be on the first Monday in December, unless they shall by law appoint a different day." — Art. I. § 4. 2.

3. *Who are to judge of the elections, returns, and qualifications of members?*

"Each house shall be the judge of the elections, returns, and qualifications of its own members." — Art. I. § 5. 1.

4. *Suppose two persons from the same district claim that they have been elected representatives for that district?*

The house decides which is entitled to a seat.

5. *How large a number of each house constitutes a quorum?*

"A majority of each shall constitute a quorum to do business." — Art. I. § 5. 1.

6. *Suppose there is not a majority present?*

"A smaller number may adjourn from day to day, and may be authorized to compel the attendance of absent members, in such a manner, and under such penalties, as each house may provide." — Art. I. § 5. 1.

7. *Who determine the rules of proceeding in each house?*

"Each house may determine the rules of its proceedings, punish its members for disorderly conduct, and, with the concurrence of two thirds, expel a member." — Art. I. § 5. 2.

8. *What are the rules adopted by legislative bodies for transacting business called?*

Parliamentary law.

9. *When is a man said to be unparliamentary?*

When he does not observe parliamentary rules.

10. *What does the Constitution require in regard to a journal?*

"Each house shall keep a journal of its proceedings, and from time to time publish the same, excepting such parts as may in their judgment require secrecy." — Art. I. § 5. 3.

11. *When must the yeas and nays be entered on the journal?*

"The yeas and nays of the members of either house on any question shall, at the desire of one fifth of those present, be entered on the journal." — Art. I. § 5. 3.

12. *Why was this provision?*

That it may be known how every member votes on a question.

13. *What evil may result from this provision?*

A factious minority may, by calling for the yeas and nays on every question, needlessly consume time and impede legislation.

14. *What is the provision in regard to adjournment?*

"Neither house, during the session of Congress, shall, without the consent of the other, adjourn for more than three days, nor to any other place than that in which the two houses shall be sitting." — Art. I. § 5. 4.

15. *Do the members of Congress receive compensation for their services?*

"The senators and representatives shall receive a compensation for their services, to be ascertained by law, and paid out of the treasury of the United States." — Art. I. § 6. 1.

16. *What compensation do they now [1867] receive?*

Five thousand dollars a year, and eight dollars for every twenty miles travelled in going to and returning from the seat of government.

17. *What are the constitutional privileges of members of Congress?*

"They shall, in all cases, except treason, felony, and breach of the peace, be privileged from arrest during their attendance at the session of their respective houses, and in going to and returning from the same; and for any speech or debate in either house, they shall not be questioned in any other place." — Art. I. § 6. 1.

18. *Why is this privilege from arrest given?*

That the constituents may not be deprived of the services of their representative.

19. *Suppose a member uses language in the house which would subject him to prosecution if uttered elsewhere?*

He cannot be called to account for it elsewhere.

20. *Why is he thus protected?*

In order that there may be perfect freedom of speech in debate.

21. *To what offices are senators and representatives ineligible?*

"No senator or representative shall, during the time for which he was elected, be appointed to any civil office under the authority of the United States, which shall have been created, or the emoluments whereof shall have been increased, during such time." — Art. I. § 6. 2.

22. *What is the object of this provision?*
To prevent corruption on the part of members of Congress.

23. *Can any one holding an office under the United States be a member of Congress?*
"No person holding any office under the United States shall be a member of either house during his continuance in office." — Art. I. § 6. 2.

24. *Suppose an officer in the army is elected to Congress?*
He must resign his commission before he can take his seat.

25. *Why is this required?*
That the different departments of government may be kept distinct.

CHAPTER XI.

MODE OF PASSING LAWS.

1. *Where must revenue bills originate?*
"All bills for raising revenue shall originate in the House of Representatives; but the Senate may propose or concur with amendments as on other bills." — Art. I. § 7. 1.

2. *What reason can be given for this?*
It may be said that the representatives are more closely connected with the people who pay the taxes, and therefore, bills for laying taxes should originate with them.

3. *What is done with a bill when it has passed both houses of Congress?*

"Every bill which shall have passed the House of Representatives and the Senate, shall, before it become a law, be presented to the President of the United States. If he approves, he shall sign it; but if not, he shall return it, with his objections, to that house in which it shall have originated, who shall enter the objections at large on their journal, and proceed to reconsider it. If, after such reconsideration, two thirds of that house shall agree to pass the bill, it shall be sent, together with the objections, to the other house, by which it shall be likewise reconsidered, and if approved by two thirds of that house, it shall become a law." — Art. I. § 7. 2.

4. *How shall the votes in such cases be determined?*

"In all such cases the votes of both houses shall be determined by yeas and nays, and the names of the persons voting for and against the bill shall be entered on the journal of each house respectively." — Art. I. § 7. 2.

5. *In what other way may a bill become a law without the signature of the President?*

"If any bill shall not be returned by the President within ten days (Sundays excepted) after it shall have been presented to him, the same shall be a law in like manner as if he had signed it, unless the Congress by their adjournment prevent its return, in which case it shall not be a law." — Art. I. § 7. 2.

6. *What must be done with every order, resolution, or vote of the Senate and House of Representatives?*

"Every order, resolution, or vote, to which the concurrence of the Senate and House of Representatives may be necessary (except on a question of adjournment), shall be presented to the President of the United States; and before the same shall take effect, shall be approved by him, or being disapproved by him, shall be repassed by two thirds of the Senate and House of Representatives, according to the rules and limitations prescribed in the case of a bill." — Art. I. § 7. 3.

7. *What is the object of this provision?*

To prevent Congress from passing a law, under the name of an order or resolution, without the consent of the President.

8. *What is the power of the President to negative laws called?*

The veto power.

9. *Why should he possess it?*

It is an additional security against the enactment of rash and improper laws.

10. *Can the President defeat a measure that is of vital importance to the country?*

He can, unless two thirds of both houses vote to pass it.

QUESTIONS FOR REVIEW.

NATURE OF THE CONSTITUTION, ETC.

1. Is the Constitution a league of sovereign states?
2. What was it designed to form? *Ans.* A national government?
3. By whom was it ordained and established?
4. By whom can it be changed or abolished?
5. Who is to decide as to the constitutionality of acts of Congress?

6. How are the powers of government divided by the Constitution?

7. What is the duty of the legislative department?

8. What is the duty of the judicial department?

9. What is the duty of the executive department?

10. Where is the legislative power placed by the Constitution?

11. How is Congress composed?

12. Why are two houses of Congress better than one?

13. How is the House of Representatives composed?

14. What are the qualifications of members?

15. How are representatives apportioned among the states?

16. What is the present ratio of representation?

17. Suppose a state has less than that number of inhabitants?

18. What is done when vacancies occur in the representation from any state?

19. Who presides over the House of Representatives?

20. W[illegible]ide cases of contested elections?

21. Who decide cases of contested elections in the Senate?

22. Where is the power of impeachment vested?

23. What is an impeachment?

24. By whom are impeachments tried?

25. How is the Senate composed?

26. Why are senators chosen for a longer time than representatives?

27. Why do not all the senators go out of office at the same time?

28. What are the qualifications for senators?

29. Who is the presiding officer of the Senate?

30. Suppose vacancies occur in the representation of a state?

31. What judicial power does the Senate possess?

32. Who would preside if the President of the United States should be tried?

33. What punishment can follow conviction on impeachment?

34. How often must Congress meet?

35. What constitutes a quorum of each house?

36. When may the yeas and nays be called for?

37. What is the compensation of members of Congress?

38. What are the privileges of members?

39. To what offices are they ineligible?

40. May a member of Congress hold any office under the government of the United States.

41. May an officer in the army have a seat in Congress?

42. State the mode of passing laws?

43. What is done if the President refuses to sign a bill?

44. What is the veto power?

CHAPTER XII.

POWERS OF CONGRESS.

1. *What is the power of Congress in respect to taxation?*

"Congress shall have power to lay and collect taxes, duties, imposts, and excises, to pay the debts and provide for the common defence and general welfare of the United States; but all duties, imposts, and excises shall be uniform throughout the United States." — Art. I. § 8. 1.

2. *What are duties and imposts?*

Taxes levied on goods upon their importation from a foreign country.

3. *What are excises?*

Taxes levied upon goods manufactured, or sold, or used in a country.

4. *For what objects is it here stated that taxes may be laid?*

"To pay the debts and provide for the common defence and general welfare of the United States."

5. *Has Congress power to lay duties in order to protect and foster domestic manufactures?*

Repeated decisions of the Supreme Court have settled this question in the affirmative.

6. *What is the second power of Congress mentioned in the eighth section of the first Article of the Constitution?*

"To borrow money on the credit of the United States."

7. *Why is Congress empowered to borrow money?*

Because there are times — especially when the country is engaged in war — when the expenses would be too great to be met by the usual means of income with sufficient promptness.

8. *What is the third power?*

"To regulate commerce with foreign nations, and among the several states, and with the Indian tribes."

9. *Why should Congress possess this power?*

In order to prevent encroachments on our commerce by foreign nations, and in order that the regulations may be uniform throughout the United States.

10. *What is a tariff?*

A law imposing duties or taxes on goods imported from foreign countries.

11. *What is a revenue tariff?*

A tariff having for its sole object the raising of money for the government.

12. *What is a protective tariff?*

A tariff which has for its object the encouragement of domestic products and manufactures.

13. *How are tariff duties collected?*

The law requires all foreign goods to be landed at certain ports, called ports of entry, and at every port of entry a collector is appointed to receive the duties levied by law on goods imported.

14. *What is a custom-house?*

The custom-house is the building in which the collector and his assistants transact the business of the revenue.

15. *What is the fourth power?*

"To establish a uniform rule of naturalization, and uniform laws on the subject of bankruptcies, through out the United States."

16. *What are naturalization laws?*

Laws regulating the manner in which foreigners may become citizens of the United States.

17. *How may a foreigner become a citizen?*

He must go before a court, and declare upon oath his intention to become a citizen.

18. *How long before his admission as a citizen must this declaration be made?*

Two years.

19. *What must he do at the end of the two years?*

He must go before the court and take an oath to support the Constitution, and renounce his allegiance to all other governments.

20. *How long must he live in the United States before he can become a citizen?*

Five years.

21. *What are bankrupt laws?*

Laws discharging insolvent debtors from the legal obligation to pay their debts.

22. *What is the fifth power?*

"To coin money, regulate the value thereof, and of foreign coin, and fix the standard of weights and measures."

23. *Why was this power given to Congress?*

In order that the coin and the standard of weights and measures may be uniform throughout the United States.

24. *What is the sixth power?*

"To provide for the punishment of counterfeiting the securities and current coin of the United States."

25. *What is the seventh power?*

"To establish post offices and post roads."

26. *Why was this power given?*

In no other way could a harmonious postal system embracing all the states be secured.

27. *What is the eighth power?*

"To promote the progress of science and the useful arts, by securing for limited times to authors and inventors the exclusive right to their respective writings and discoveries."

28. *What laws have been passed under this power?*

Copyright and patent laws.

29. *What is a copyright law?*

A law securing for a limited time to authors the exclusive right to publish and sell their works in the United States.

30. *For what length of time does the law now in force secure to authors this right?*

Twenty-eight years.

31. *What is a patent law?*

A law securing for a limited time to inventors the exclusive right to manufacture and sell the invention in the United States.

32. *What is the ninth power?*

"To constitute tribunals inferior to the Supreme Court."

33. *What is the tenth power?*

"To define and punish piracies and felonies committed on the high seas, and offences against the law of nations."

34. *What is the eleventh power?*

"To declare war, grant letters of marque and reprisal, and make rules concerning captures on land and water."

35. *What are letters of marque and reprisal?*

Commissions granted by a government to one or more of its citizens to seize the property of an enemy.

36. *What are vessels sailing under such commissions called?*

Privateers.

CHAPTER XIII.

POWERS OF CONGRESS CONTINUED.

1. *What is the twelfth power conferred on Congress by the Constitution?*

"To raise and support armies; but no appropriation of money to that use shall be for a longer term than two years."

2. *Why this restriction in regard to time?*

That the people, if they do not approve of the war, may put an end to it by electing new representatives who will refuse to vote money for carrying it on.

3. *What are the thirteenth and fourteenth powers?*

"To provide and maintain a navy; to make rules for the government and regulation of the land and naval forces."

4. *What is the fifteenth power?*

"To provide for calling forth the militia to execute the laws of the Union, suppress insurrections, and repel invasions."

5. *What is the sixteenth power?*

"To provide for organizing, arming, and disciplining the militia, and for governing such part of them as may be employed in the service of the United States, reserving to the states respectively the appointment of the officers, and the authority of training the militia according to the discipline prescribed by Congress."

6. *Why should Congress have power to prescribe the rules for training the militia?*

That there may be that uniformity of organization and discipline which is necessary to the highest efficiency when called into active service.

7. *Why is the right to appoint the officers of the militia reserved to the states?*

To prevent jealousy of the general government on the part of the state governments.

8. *Wherein does the regular army of the United States differ from the militia?*

The regular army consists of men enlisted and officered by the authority of the United States, and are under its exclusive control; while the militia are under the control of the several states, except when called into the service of the United States.

9. *What is the power of Congress over the District of Columbia?*

"To exercise exclusive legislation, in all cases whatsoever, over such district (not exceeding ten miles square) as may, by cession of particular states and the acceptance of Congress, become the seat of government of the United States, and to exercise like authority over all places purchased by the consent of the legislature of the state in which the same shall be, for the erection of forts, magazines, arsenals, dock-yards, and other needful buildings." — Art. I. § 8. 17.

10. *What can be said in favor of these provisions?*

Complete control of the seat of government is necessary to the independence of Congress, and the property of the Union should not be subject to the control of any one of the states.

11. *What is the eighteenth power mentioned?*

"To make all laws necessary and proper for carrying into execution the foregoing powers, and all other powers vested by this Constitution in the government of the United States, or in any department or officer thereof." — Art. I. § 8. 18.

12. *Has Congress power to charter a national bank or banks?*

It has. A national bank was chartered during the first administration of Washington, and another during the administration of Madison.

13. *Was the constitutionality of those acts questioned?*

It was; but two decisions of the Supreme Court settled the question in the affirmative.

14. *When were the national banks now in existence chartered?*

They are the result of "An Act to provide a national currency, secured by a pledge of United States stocks, and to provide for the circulation and redemption thereof," passed by Congress in 1863.

QUESTIONS FOR REVIEW.

POWERS OF CONGRESS.

1. What is the power of Congress limited by?
2. What is the power of Congress as to taxation?
3. Can it lay and collect taxes for any object whatever?
4. Could the Congress of the Confederation lay and collect taxes?
5. What are duties and imposts?
6. What are excises?
7. Can Congress impose higher duties at New York than at Boston?
8. Why not?
9. Where are duties collected?
10. Who can borrow money on the credit of the United States?
11. What does the money thus borrowed constitute? *Ans.* The national debt.
12. Who can regulate foreign and domestic commerce?
13. Had the Congress of the Confederation power to regulate commerce?
14. Have the state governments this power?
15. What duties can the state legislatures lay? See Art. I. § 10. 2.
16. What is a tariff?
17. What is a revenue tariff?

18. What is a protective tariff?

19. Can Congress pass a protective tariff?

20. What is an alien?

21. How can foreigners become citizens?

22. What are bankrupt laws!

23. Who have power to pass such laws?

24. Who can coin money?

25. Can the states coin money?

26. Why is the power to coin money and fix the standard of weights and measures exclusive with Congress?

27. Who can establish post offices and post roads?

28. Can a state establish a postal system within its limits?

29. What are copyright laws?

30. What are patent laws?

31. Why is the power to pass such laws vested in Congress?

32. By whom may war be declared?

33. For how long a time may appropriations of money for carrying it on be made?

34. Why this restriction?

35. Can the Senate introduce a bill for revenue?

36. Can it introduce all other bills?

37. Where is the power to build a navy placed?

38. What are letters of marque?

39. Can a state grant letters of marque?

40. When can the militia be called out by the United States?

41. Can the militia be called out by the executive of a state to execute the state laws?

42. Over what territory has Congress exclusive jurisdiction?

43. Can Congress charter a national bank?

44. Has the Supreme Court decided this question?

CHAPTER XIV.

PROHIBITIONS ON THE UNITED STATES.

1. *Why does the Constitution contain prohibitions on the United States?*

As the national government is one of limited powers, it is proper to state what it cannot do.

2. *Repeat the paragraph of the Constitution relating to the slave trade.*

"The migration or importation of such persons as any of the states now existing shall think proper to admit shall not be prohibited by Congress prior to the year one thousand eight hundred and eight; but a tax or duty may be imposed on such importation, not exceeding ten dollars for each person." — Art. I. § 9. 1.

3. *Did some of the framers of the Constitution wish to abolish the slave trade at once?*

They did. Among them were some of the leading statesmen of Virginia and other southern states.

4. *When was it abolished?*

A law was passed in 1804, prohibiting its continuance after 1808.

5. *When may the writ of habeas corpus be suspended?*

"The privilege of the writ of *habeas corpus* shall not be suspended, unless when, in cases of rebellion or invasion, the public safety may require it." — Art. I. § 10. 2.

6. *What is meant by a writ of habeas corpus?*

It is an order, issued by a judge or court, commanding the person having another in custody or in prison, to bring the prisoner before him. If the prisoner is illegally or improperly in custody, the judge will discharge him.

7. *What is the great value of the habeas corpus?*

It is a safeguard against illegal imprisonment.

8. *By whom may the writ of habeas corpus be suspended?*

The Constitution does not say. During the late rebellion it was suspended by the President, and his act was afterwards sanctioned by Congress.

9. *What is a bill of attainder?*

An act of the legislature inflicting capital punishment on persons supposed to be guilty of high offences, such as treason and felony, without any trial by a court of justice.

10. *What is an ex post facto law?*

A law making an act criminal which was not criminal when it was performed.

11. *Can Congress pass such laws?*

"No bill of attainder, or *ex post facto* law, shall be passed." — Art. I. § 9. 3.

12. *Why this prohibition?*

Because great injustice could be done if an act, which was not a crime when it was performed, could afterwards be declared to be a crime.

13. *What is the restriction as to taxes?*

"No capitation or other direct tax shall be laid, unless in proportion to the census or enumeration hereinbefore directed to be taken." — Art. I. § 9. 4.

14. *What is a capitation tax?*

A poll . that is, a uniform tax on individuals without regard to the unequal value of their property.

15. *What is said respecting taxes on exports?*

"No tax or duty shall be laid on articles exported from any state. No preference shall be given, by any regulation of commerce or revenue, to the ports of one state over another; nor shall vessels bound to or from one state be obliged to enter, clear, or pay duties in another." — Art. I. § 9. 5.

16. *What was the design of these provisions?*

To give a national character to the Union of the states by forbidding state preferences or superiorities.

17. *Can Congress lay an export duty on cotton?*

It cannot, for it cannot lay a tax on any article exported from any state.

18. *Can Congress lay a tax of any kind upon cotton?*

It can lay a tax on its production, just as it can lay a tax on the production of any other article.

19. *Give an example of a tax on production.*

Congress has laid a tax on every gallon of whiskey distilled, and on every gallon of oil refined; and so it may lay a tax on every bale of cotton produced or sold.

20. *What is said respecting drawing money from the treasury?*

"No money shall be drawn from the treasury but in consequence of appropriations made by law; and a regular statement and account of the receipts and expenditures of all public money shall be published from time to time." — Art. I. § 9. 6.

21. *Who has thus the general control of the public purse?*

Congress.

22. *Who has the immediate control of it?*

The Secretary of the Treasury.

23. *Who has the money of the United States in his keeping?*

The Treasurer of the United States.

24. *Where is the Treasury?*

At Washington.

25. *Is all the money of the United States kept at Washington?*

There are Sub-Treasuries and Sub-Treasurers in the principal cities of the Union.

26. *Why must an account of the receipts and expenditures be published?*

In order that the people may know what is done with their money.

27. *What is said respecting titles of nobility?*

"No title of nobility shall be granted by the United States; and no person holding any office of profit or trust under them shall, without the consent of Congress, accept of any present, emolument, office, or title of any kind whatsoever from any king, prince, or foreign state." — Art. I. § 9. 7.

28. *What was the design of these provisions?*

To preserve the equality of citizens necessary in a republic, and to guard against foreign influence over the public servants of the United States.

CHAPTER XV.

PROHIBITIONS ON THE STATES.

1. *Why are there prohibitions on the states?*

To prevent them from interfering with the operations of the national government when exercising the powers conferred on it by the Constitution.

2. *What are some of the prohibitions on the states?*

"No state shall enter into any treaty, alliance, or confederation; grant letters of marque and reprisal; coin money; emit bills of credit; make anything but gold and silver coin a legal tender in payment of debts; pass any bill of attainder, *ex post facto* law, or law impairing the obligation of contracts; or grant any title of nobility." — Art. I. § 10. 1.

3. *What are bills of credit?*

Notes issued by the government intended to circulate as money.

4. *What does this clause of the Constitution prohibit?*

It prohibits the emission of any paper medium by a state government for the purpose of common circulation.

5. *Can Congress make anything but gold and silver coin a legal tender for the payment of debts?*

The Constitution does not forbid Congress to do it.*

---

* An act of Congress, passed 1862, made United States treasury notes a legal tender.

6. *What is meant by impairing the obligation of contracts?*

Any law which enlarges, abridges, or in any manner changes the intention of the parties who made it.

7. *How extensive is the meaning of the term "contract" as here used?*

It includes legislative grants, charters, and compacts between states.

8. *Can a state pass a bankrupt law?*

It cannot.

9. *Why not?*

Because such a law would be one impairing the obligation of contracts.

10. *What laws in relation to discharging the obligation of debtors may a state pass?*

Laws discharging such contracts only as are made after the passing of such laws, and such as are made within the state between citizens of the same state.

11. *Mention some further prohibitions on the states.*

"No state shall, without the consent of Congress, lay any imposts or duties on imports or exports, except what may be absolutely necessary for executing its inspection laws." — Art. I. § 10. 2

12. *What are inspection laws?*

Laws requiring goods to be examined by public officers, that their quality may be ascertained?

13. *Suppose such duties are laid by a state.*

"The net produce of all duties and imposts laid by any state on imports or exports shall be for the use of the treasury of the United States; and all such laws shall be subject to the revision and control of Congress." — Art. I. § 10. 2.

14. *What prohibitions are there in regard to tonnage, troops, etc.?*

"No state shall, without the consent of Congress, lay any duty on tonnage, keep troops or ships of war in time of peace, enter into any agreement or compact with another state, or with a foreign power, or engage in war, unless actually invaded, or in such imminent danger as will not admit of delay." — Art. I. § 10. 2.

15. *What is a tonnage duty?*

A tax laid upon vessels in proportion to their tonnage.

16. *What can be said in favor of these restrictions on the states?*

They are necessary, in order that there may be no interference by the states with the exercise of those powers of the national government which relate to the common interests of all the states.

17. *What is one of the characteristic powers of a sovereign state?*

The power to make treaties with other states and nations.

18. *Does any one of the United States possess this power?*

No; because the Constitution says, "No state shall enter into any agreement or compact with another state or a foreign power."

QUESTIONS FOR REVIEW.

PROHIBITIONS ON CONGRESS AND THE STATES.

1. Was the slave trade in operation when the Constitution was formed?
2. How long did the Constitution permit it to exist?
3. What is the writ of *habeas corpus?*
4. When may it be suspended?
5. What is the effect of such suspension?
6. What is a bill of attainder?
7. What is an *ex post facto* law?
8. Why is Congress prohibited from passing such laws?
9. Can Congress lay a tax on exports?
10. Can a state lay such a tax?
11. In what way may Congress lay a tax upon cotton?
12. Can Congress give the ports of one state any advantages over those of another?
13. Why not?
14. How can money be drawn from the United States treasury?
15. Who has the general charge of the finances of the government?
16. Who has the immediate charge of the public money?
17. What is a Sub-Treasury?
18. Can Congress confer any title of nobility?
19. Who confers titles of nobility in Great Britain? *Ans.* The king.
20. Can an ambassador to England accept a present from the queen?
21. Why not?
22. What is a legal tender?
23. What only can the states make a legal tender?
24. Can the United States make anything else a legal tender?
25. What have they made a legal tender?

26. Can a state issue treasury notes to circulate as money?
27. Can a state form a league with another state or states?
28. What clause in the Constitution forbids it?
29. Can the legislature pass a law declaring a man guilty of a crime, and inflict punishment upon him?
30. Why not?
31. Suppose a man has contracted a debt, can the legislature of a state release him from the legal obligation to pay it?
32. Why not?
33. Do not the states pass insolvent laws?
34. What debts do they affect?
35. Could the state of New York enter into an agreement with the British government respecting flour shipped from New York?
36. Why not?
37. When can a state raise troops and engage in war?

CHAPTER XVI.

THE EXECUTIVE DEPARTMENT.—ELECTION OF THE PRESIDENT.

1. *What is the duty of the executive department?*

To execute the laws.

2. *Where is the executive power vested?*

"The executive power shall be vested in a President of the United States of America. He shall hold office during the term of four years."—Art. II. § 1. 1.

3. *How are the President and Vice-President chosen?*

"Each state shall appoint, in such manner as the legislature thereof may direct, a number of electors equal to the whole number of senators and representatives to which each state may be entitled in Congress; but no senator or representative, or person holding an office of trust or profit under the United States, shall be appointed an elector." — Art. II. § 1. 2.

4. *In what manner do the electors proceed to make the election?*

"The electors shall meet in their respective states, and vote by ballot for President and Vice-President, one of whom, at least, shall not be an inhabitant of the same state with themselves; they shall name in their ballots the person voted for as President, and in distinct ballots the person voted for as Vice-President; and they shall make distinct lists of all persons voted for as President, and of all persons voted for as Vice-President, and of the number of votes for each, which lists they shall sign, and certify, and transmit, sealed, to the seat of government of the United States, directed to the President of the Senate; the President of the Senate shall, in the presence of the Senate and the House of Representatives, open all the certificates, and the votes shall then be counted; the person having the greatest number of votes for President shall be President, if such number be a majority of the whole number of electors appointed; and if no person shall have such majority, then, from the persons having the highest numbers, not exceeding three, on the list of those voted for as President, the House of Representatives shall choose immediately, by ballot, the President. But in choosing the President, the votes shall be taken by states, the representation from each state having one vote; a quorum for this purpose shall consist of a member or members of two thirds of the states, and a majority of all the states shall be necessary to a choice. And if the House of Representatives shall not choose a President, whenever the right of choice shall devolve upon them, before the fourth of March next following, then the Vice-President shall act as President, as in case of the death or other constitutional disability of the President." — Amend. Art. XII. 1.

5. *What is said as to the Vice-President?*

"The person having the greatest number of votes as Vice-President shall be the Vice-President, if such number be a majority of the whole number of electors appointed; and if no person have a majority, then, from the two highest on the list, the Senate shall choose the Vice-President: a quorum for the purpose shall consist of two thirds of the whole number of senators, and a majority of the whole number shall be necessary to a choice." — Amend. Art. XII. 2.

"But no person constitutionally ineligible to the office of President shall be eligible to that of Vice-President of the United States." — Amend. Art. XII. 3.

6. *Is this the orginal method prescribed by the Constitution for choosing the President and Vice-President?*

It is not, but is the result of an Amendment to the Constitution, proposed by Congress in October, 1803, and ratified before September, 1804.

7. *What is the provision of the Constitution in regard to the choice of electors?*

"The Congress may determine the time of choosing the electors, and the day on which they shall give their votes; which day shall be the same throughout the United States." — Art. II. § 1. 4.

5

8. *Why was this power conferred upon Congress?*

That the time of choosing electors may be the same throughout the Union.

9. *Why is this desirable?*

It has a tendency to repress political intrigues and corruption.

10. *How does that appear?*

Suppose the electors for President were to vote in different states at different times, and that the electors of all the states except one had voted, and that the result of the election depended upon the vote of that state, great efforts would be made to secure the vote of that state.

CHAPTER XVII.

ELECTION OF PRESIDENT AND VICE-PRESIDENT, CONTINUED.

1. *What states have the advantage when the President is chosen by the electors?*

The most populous states, as they have more electoral votes than the smaller states.

2. *What happens when the choice devolves on the House of Representatives?*

Each state has then an equal voice in the choice of the President, because the house votes by states.

3. *How many times has the choice devolved on the house?*

Twice. Jefferson's first election was by the house, and John Quincy Adams was chosen by the house.

4. *What are the qualifications of the President?*

"No person except a natural born citizen, or a citizen of the United States at the time of the adoption of this Constitution, shall be eligible to the office of President; neither shall any person be eligible to that office who shall not have attained to the age of thirty-five years, and been fourteen years a resident within the United States." — Art. II. § 1. 5.

5. *Suppose a man has lived abroad several years in the service of his country?*

That would not interrupt his residence so as to disqualify him for the office of President.

6. *How often may the President be reëlected?*

As often as the people please.

7. *What is done in case of the inability or death of the President, or his removal from office?*

"In case of the removal of the President from office, or of his death, resignation, or inability to discharge the powers and duties of the said office, the same shall devolve on the Vice-President; and the Congress may by law provide for the case of removal, death, resignation, or inability both of the President and Vice-President, declaring what officer shall then act as President; and such officer shall act accordingly until the disability be removed, or a President shall be elected." — Art. II. § 1. 6.

8. *In what cases has the Vice-President succeeded to the office of President?*

By the death of William Henry Harrison, John Tyler became President; by the death of Zachary Taylor, Millard Fillmore; and by the death of Abraham Lincoln, Andrew Johnson.

9. *What officer has Congress declared shall act as President in case of the removal, death, or resignation both of the President and Vice-President?*

Congress has provided that the President *pro tempore* of the Senate shall act as President, and in case there is no president *pro tempore*, the Speaker of the House of Representatives.

10. *What provision does the Constitution make for the compensation of the President?*

"The President shall, at stated times, receive for his services a compensation which shall neither be increased nor diminished during the period for which he shall have been elected, and he shall not receive within that period any other emolument from the United States, or any of them." — Art. II. § 1. 7.

11. *What is the salary of the President as fixed by Congress?*

Twenty-five thousand dollars a year were voted by the first Congress under the Constitution, and the amount has never been changed.

12. *What oath or affirmation must the President take before entering on the execution of his office?*

"I do solemnly swear (or affirm) that I will faithfully execute the office of President of the United States, and will, to the best of my ability, preserve, protect, and defend the Constitution of the United States." — Art. II. § 1. 8.

CHAPTER XVIII.

DUTIES OF THE PRESIDENT.

1. *What military power does the President possess?*

"The President shall be commander-in-chief of the army and navy of the United States, and of the militia of the several states when called into the actual service of the United States." — Art. II. § 2. 1.

2. *What may he require of the heads of departments?*

"He may require the opinion in writing of the principal officer in each of the executive departments upon any subject relating to the duties of their respective offices." —Art. II. § 2. 1.

3. *What power has he with respect to reprieves and pardons?*

"He shall have power to grant reprieves and pardons for offences against the United States, except in cases of impeachment." — Art. II. § 2. 1.

4. *What is the design of the pardoning power?*

It is designed to promote justice and the public good.

5. *In what way can it promote justice?*

Men are sometimes convicted of crimes when they are innocent, and they must suffer wrongfully unless delivered by the pardoning power.

6. *Why may not the President pardon those who have been impeached and found guilty?*

It would be in his power to shield his favorites from punishment, however great might be their political offences.

7. *What is his power with respect to treaties?*

"He shall have power, by and with the advice and consent of the Senate, to make treaties, provided two thirds of the senators present concur." — Art. II. § 2. 2.

8. *What is the usual method of making treaties?*

Treaties are negotiated on the part of the United States by the Secretary of State, or by a foreign minister under instructions from the Secretary. When the treaty is completed, it is sent to the President, who lays it before the Senate. If two thirds of the senators present approve it, he may give it his signature, when it becomes a part of the supreme law of the land.

9. *May the President withhold his signature after the Senate has approved the treaty?*

He may.

10. *When a treaty has been approved by the Senate and signed by the President, and money is wanted to carry it into execution, is the House of Representatives bound to vote the money needed, even if they do not approve the treaty?*

They are. The power of making and ratifying treaties belongs to the President and Senate.

11. *What is the President's power of appointment to office?*

"He shall nominate, and by and with the advice and consent of the Senate, shall appoint Ambassadors, other public Ministers and Consuls, Judges of the Supreme Court, and all other officers of the United States, whose appointments are not herein otherwise provided for, and which shall be established by law." — Art. II. § 2. 2.

12. *Are all the officers of the United States appointed by the President and Senate?*

No. "The Congress may by law vest the appointment of such inferior officers as they think proper in the President alone, in the courts of law or in the heads of departments." — Art. II. § 2. 2.

13. *Suppose vacancies occur during the recess of the Senate.*

"The President shall have power to fill all vacancies that may happen during the recess of the Senate by granting commissions which shall expire at the end of their next session." — Art. II. § 2. 3.

14. *Where is the power of removal from office vested by the Constitution?*

The Constitution is silent on the subject of removals except by impeachment.

15. *By whom has the power of removal always been exercised?*

By the President alone.

16. *What is required of the President in relation to Congress?*

"He shall from time to time give to the Congress information of the state of the Union, and recommend to their consideration such measures as he shall judge necessary and expedient." — Art. II. § 3. 1.

17. *Why should he do this?*

Because he may have important information not possessed by Congress, especially in relation to foreign affairs.

18. *Does the President communicate with Congress orally or by message?*

By message.

19. *Is Congress obliged to consider the recommendations made by the President?*

No.

20. *Has the President power to call extra sessions of Congress?*

"He may on extraordinary occasions convene both houses, or either of them." — Art. II. § 3. 1.

21. *What power of adjourning Congress does the President possess?*

"In case of disagreement between them with respect to the time of adjournment, he may adjourn them to such time as he shall think proper." — Art. II. § 3. 1.

22. *What is the duty of the President as to foreign ministers?*

"He shall receive ambassadors and other public ministers." — Art. II. § 3. 1.

23. *Is this an important power?*

It is; for it gives the President a great degree of power in determining the relations of the United States to other nations.

24. *Suppose a colony of a country rebels and sets up a new government, and the President receives their ambassador, what would be the effect of such reception?*

It would be an acknowledgment of the independence of the rebels by the United States.

25. *What might this acknowledgment occasion?*

War with the parent state.

26. *What is the duty of the President in regard to the laws?*

"He shall take care that the laws be faithfully executed, and shall commission all the officers of the United States."—Art. II. § 3. 1.

27. *How may the President and other officers be removed from office?*

"The President, Vice-President, and all civil officers of the United States shall be removed from office on impeachment for, and conviction of, treason, bribery, or other high crimes or misdemeanors." — Art. II. § 4. 1.

28. *How are military officers tried?*

They are tried by a court martial, which is a court composed of military officers detailed for that purpose by the commanding officer.

29. *How many executive departments have been constituted by Congress?*

Five, viz., the department of state or foreign affairs, of the interior, of the treasury, of war, and of the navy.

30. *Who constitute the cabinet?*

The heads of departments, together with the attorney-general and the postmaster-general.

QUESTIONS FOR REVIEW.

THE EXECUTIVE.

1. What is the duty of the executive?
2. Have the United States a single or plural executive?
3. Where is the executive power vested?
4. Where was the executive power of the Republic of Rome vested? *Ans.* In two consuls.
5. Where is the executive power of Great Britain vested?
6. How is the President elected?
7. Under what circumstances does the election devolve upon the House of Representatives?

8. How is the vote then taken?

9. What Presidents were chosen by the House of Representatives?

10. Who choose the Vice-President when there is no choice by the electors?

11. For what length of time is the President chosen?

12. How often may he be reëlected?

13. Has any President served for more than two terms?

14. What are the qualifications for President?

15. Could a foreigner have been elected President when the Constitution was adopted?

16. Can a foreigner be elected now?

17. Why not?

18. When the office of President becomes vacant, who succeeds to it?

19. Suppose there is no Vice-President; who is to exercise the office of President?

20. Suppose there is no President *pro tempore?*

21. Does the Constitution say that the President of the Senate *pro tempore*, or the Speaker of the House, shall exercise the office of President?

22. By what provision are they to exercise the office in certain circumstances?

23. Who is commander-in-chief of the army and navy?

24. Who has the superintendence and general control of all matters pertaining to the army?

25. Who has immediate command of all the armies of the United States? *Ans.* The general.

26. Who appoints and commissions all important military and civil officers?

27. Suppose the Senate is not in session when the vacancy occurs?

28. Who has the power of removal from office?

29. How are treaties made?

30. How is war declared?

31. How may extra sessions of Congress be called?

32. Who receives ambassadors and other public ministers?

33. Show that this is an important power.

34. What is the duty of the President with respect to executing the laws?

35. Suppose the people of a state refuse to obey the laws of the United States?

36. Can a state be coerced into obedience? *Ans.* All men, wherever found within the limits of the United States, can be compelled to render obedience to the laws.

37. How can the President be removed from office?

38. How can the Vice-President and all civil officers of the United States be removed from office?

39. Are members of Congress civil officers of the United States, and liable to impeachment?

40. How can a member be removed from either house of Congress before his term has expired?

CHAPTER XIX.

THE JUDICIAL DEPARTMENT.

1. *Where is the judicial power vested?*

"The judicial power of the United States shall be vested in one Supreme Court, and in such inferior courts as the Congress may from time to time ordain and establish."—Art. III. § 1. 1.

2. *How many national courts have been established by Congress?*

Three: the Supreme Court, the Circuit Court, and the District Court.

3. *Of what does the Supreme Court consist?*

The Supreme Court consists of a Chief Justice and nine associate justices, any five of whom constitute a quorum.

4. *How often does the Supreme Court hold its sessions?*

It holds one term annually, commencing on the first Monday in December, at Washington.

5. *How is it chiefly occupied?*

In hearing and deciding appeals from the Circuit and District Courts.

6. *Into how many judicial circuits are the United States divided?*

The United States are divided into ten circuits, and into a much larger number of districts.

7. *Who act as judges of the Circuit Courts?*

The associate justices of the Supreme Court.

8. *How many district judges are there?*

There is a district judge appointed in and for each district.

9. *How often are the Circuit Courts held?*

In most of the circuits, two courts are held annually.

10. *How often are the District Courts held?*

In most of the districts, the judge holds four stated terms, and also holds special courts at his discretion.

11. *What are the other officers of the national courts besides the judges?*

The attorney-general, the district attorneys, the marshals, and the clerks.

12. *What are the duties of the attorney-general and the district attorneys?*

To conduct all suits in the United States courts in which the United States are concerned.

13. *What duties has the attorney-general in connection with the cabinet?*

The attorney-general is a member of the cabinet, and meets with the other members to advise the President; he gives legal opinions on all questions submitted to him by the government.

14. *What are the duties of the marshal?*

The marshal executes the orders and decisions of the court.

15. *What are the duties of the clerks?*

To keep records of the proceedings of their courts, and sign and seal all processes.

16. *What is the tenure of office of the judges?*

"The judges, both of the supreme and inferior courts, shall hold their offices during good behavior; and shall at stated times receive for their services a compensation which shall not be diminished during their continuance in office." — Art. III. § 1. 1.

17. *Why was this tenure of office adopted?*

That the judges may be independent.

18. *How does it make them independent?*

If they held office at the will of Congress or of the President, they might be led to consult the will of Congress or of the President, rather than the dictates of justice.

19. *Who determine the compensation of the judges?*

Congress.

20. *Why cannot their compensation be diminished?*

Congress might overawe them into submission to its will by that means, thus destroying their independence and fairness.

CHAPTER XX.

JUDICIAL DEPARTMENT, CONTINUED.

1. *To what does the judicial power extend?*

"The judicial power shall extend to all cases in law and equity arising under this Constitution, the laws of the United States, and treaties made, or which shall be made, under their authority; to all cases affecting ambassadors, other public ministers, and consuls; to all cases of admiralty and maritime jurisdiction; to controversies to which the United States shall be a party; to controversies between two or more states; between a state and citizens of another state; between citizens of different states; between citizens of the same state claiming lands under grants of different states; and between a state or citizens thereof and foreign states, citizens, and subjects." — Art. III. § 2. 1.

2. *Has the Supreme Court jurisdiction in equity as well as law?*

It has.

3. *What is equity jurisprudence?*

"A system of jurisprudence, the object of which is to render the administration of justice more complete, by affording relief where the courts of law are incompetent to give it, or to give it with effect."

4. *Are not courts of equity commonly distinct from courts of law?*

They are in England and in some of the states.

5. *What are such courts called?*

Courts of chancery.

6. *What are courts of admiralty?*

Courts which have jurisdiction over cases of captures and seizures at sea, and all civil and criminal maritime cases.

7. *Have the United States courts of admiralty?*

The District Courts have admiralty powers.

8. *When has the Supreme Court original jurisdiction?*

"In all cases affecting ambassadors, other public ministers and consuls, and those in which a state shall be a party, the Supreme Court shall have original jurisdiction." — Art. III. § 2. 2.

9. *What is meant by "original jurisdiction" in these cases?*

Suits relating to them may be commenced in the first instance in the Supreme Court.

10. *How do all other cases come before the Supreme Court?*

By appeal from the Circuit Courts.

11. *What does the Constitution say on this point?*

"In all other cases before mentioned, the Supreme Court shall have appellate jurisdiction, both as to law and fact, with such exceptions, and under such regulations, as the Congress shall make." — Art. III. § 2. 2.

12. *May appeals be taken from the state courts to the national courts?*

They may. The Supreme Court has from time to time sustained the right to such appeals.

13. *What other courts are there under the control of the United States?*

There is the Supreme Court of the District of Columbia, and the courts established in the territories of the United States.

14. *Are the territorial courts regarded as a part of the national judiciary?*

They are not.

15. *Is the right of trial by jury preserved in all of these courts?*

"The trial of all crimes, except in cases of impeachment, shall be by jury; and such trial shall be held in the state where said crimes shall have been committed; but when not committed in any state, the trial shall be at such place or places as the Congress may by law have directed."—Art. III. § 2. 3.

16. *What evil is here guarded against?*

That of trying a man at a great distance from the scene of his alleged crime, and where, if innocent, it would be difficult to prove his innocence.

CHAPTER XXI.

TREASON. — FUGITIVES FROM JUSTICE. — ADMISSION OF NEW STATES.

1. *What is the definition of treason given by the Constitution?*

"Treason against the United States shall consist only in levying war against them, or in adhering to their enemies, giving them aid and comfort." — Art. III. § 3. 1.

2. *What testimony is necessary to convict one of treason?*

"No person shall be convicted of treason, unless on the testimony of two witnesses to the same overt act, or on confession in open court."—Art. III. § 3. 1.

3. *Who is to declare the punishment of treason, and how is that punishment limited?*

"Congress shall have power to declare the punishment of treason; but no attainder of treason shall work corruption of blood, or forfeiture, except during the life of the person attainted." — Art. III. § 3. 2.

4. *What punishment for treason has Congress imposed?*

Death by hanging.

5. *What is the provision of the Constitution in regard to public acts, records, &c.*

"Full faith and credit shall be given in each state to the public acts, records, and judicial proceedings of every other state, and the Congress may by general laws prescribe the manner in which such acts, records, and proceedings shall be proved, and the effect thereof." — Art. IV. § 1. 1.

6. *What privileges are guaranteed to the citizens of each state?*

"The citizens of each state shall be entitled to all the privileges and immunities of citizens in the several states." — Art. IV. § 2. 1.

7. *Does this mean that a citizen of Massachusetts is entitled, when in South Carolina, to all the rights and privileges he enjoyed in Massachusetts?*

It means that he is entitled in South Carolina to all the rights and privileges enjoyed by the citizens of that state.

8. *What is the provision of the Constitution respecting fugitives from justice?*

"A person charged in any state with treason, felony, or other crime, who shall flee from justice, and be found in another state, shall, on the demand of the executive authority of the state from which he fled, be delivered up to be removed to the state having jurisdiction of the crime." — Art. IV. § 2. 2.

9. *What is the provision respecting fugitive slaves?*

"No person held to service or labor in one state, under the laws thereof, escaping into another, shall, in consequence of any law or regulation therein, be discharged from such service or labor, but shall be delivered up on the claim of the party to whom such service or labor may be due." — Art. IV. § 2. 3.

10. *By whom may new states be admitted into the Union, and what limitations are there to the power of admission?*

"New states may be admitted by Congress into the Union; but no new state shall be formed or erected within the jurisdiction of any other state, nor any state be formed by the junction of two or more states, without the consent of the legislatures of the states concerned, as well as of Congress." — Art. IV. § 3. 1.

11. *What is the power of Congress over the territories?*

"Congress shall have power to dispose of and make all needful rules and regulations respecting the territory or other property belonging to the United States; and nothing in this Constitution shall be so construed as to prejudice any claims of the United States, or of any particular state." — Art. IV. § 3. 2.

CHAPTER XXII.

MODE OF MAKING AMENDMENTS. — SUPREMACY OF THE CONSTITUTION.

1. *What does the Constitution guarantee to every state?*

"The United States shall guarantee to every state in this Union a republican form of government, and shall protect each of them against invasion, and, on application of the legislature, or of the executive (when the legislature cannot be convened), against domestic violence." — Art. IV. § 4. 1.

2. *Suppose there should be an armed opposition to the laws of a state by a portion of the people of that state, would it be the duty of the President and of Congress to interfere?*

It would be their duty to furnish aid in enforcing the laws, on application of the legislature, or of the governor when the legislature cannot be convened.

3. *Suppose the majority of the people of a state should attempt to establish a monarchy?*

It would be the duty of the United States government to put down the attempt; for the United States are bound to guarantee to every state in the Union a republican form of government.

4. *In what ways may the Constitution be amended?*

"Congress, whenever two thirds of both houses shall deem it necessary, shall propose amendments to this Constitution; or, on the application of the legislatures of two thirds of the several states, shall call a convention for proposing amendments, which, in either case, shall be valid to all intents and purposes, as a part of this Constitution, when ratified by the legislatures of three fourths of the several states, or by conventions in three fourths thereof, as the one or the other mode of ratification may be proposed by the Congress." — Art. V. 1.

5. *State in what two ways amendments may be proposed.*

They may be proposed by Congress, or by a convention called on application of the legislatures of two thirds of the states.

6. *In what ways may the proposed amendments be ratified?*

By the legislatures of three fourths of the states, or by conventions in three fourths of the states.

7. *In what way were the amendments that have been made proposed and ratified?*

They were proposed by Congress, and ratified by the legislatures of the states.

8. *What limitations are there to the power of amendment?*

"Provided, that no amendment which may be made prior to the year one thousand eight hundred and eight shall in any manner affect the first and fourth clauses in the ninth section of the first article; and that no state, without its consent, shall be deprived of its equal suffrage in the Senate."—Art. V. 1.

9. *What do the clauses above mentioned refer to?*

To the importation of slaves, and to capitation and other direct taxes.

10. *What is said of debts contracted by the United States before the adoption of the Constitution?*

"All debts contracted and engagements entered into, before the adoption of this Constitution, shall be as valid against the United States under this Constitution, as under the Confederation." — Art. VI. 1.

11. *What is said of the supremacy of the Constitution?*

"This Constitution, and the laws of the United States which shall be made in pursuance thereof, and all treaties made, or which shall be made, under the authority of the United States, shall be the supreme law of the land; and the judges in every state shall be bound thereby, anything in the constitution and laws of any state to the contrary notwithstanding." — Art. VI. 2.

12. *What does this prohibit?*

It prohibits any state from seceding, and from making any law contrary to the Constitution and laws of the United States.

13. *What was the doctrine of nullification?*

The right claimed by some of the states to nullify an act of Congress within their borders, provided they judged the act unconstitutional.

14. *What tribunal has the Constitution made the judge as to the constitutionality of laws?*

The Supreme Court.

15. *Who are bound by oath to support the Constitution?*

"The senators and representatives before mentioned, and the members of the several state legislatures, and all executive and judicial officers, both of the United States and of the several states, shall be bound by oath or affirmation to support this Constitution." — Art. VI. 3.

16. *Is there any religious test allowed?*

"But no religious test shall ever be required as a qualification to any office or public trust under the United States." — Art. VI. 3.

QUESTIONS FOR REVIEW.

THE JUDICIARY.

1. What is the office of the judiciary?
2. Where is the judicial power of the United States vested?
3. Of what does the Supreme Court consist?
4. What are the Circuit Courts?
5. Into how many circuits are the United States divided?
6. Into how many districts are the United States divided?
7. How many district judges are there?
8. Where and how often does the Supreme Court hold its sessions?
9. To what does the judicial power extend?
10. What is meant by equity jurisprudence?
11. What are courts of equity commonly called?
12. Has the Supreme Court both original and appellate jurisdiction?
13. When does it exercise original jurisdiction? *Ans.* When suits are commenced in that court?
14. When does it exercise appellate jurisdiction?
15. In what cases has the Supreme Court original jurisdiction?
16. In what cases has it appellate jurisdiction?
17. May appeals in some cases be taken from the state to the national courts?
18. What is the tenure of office of the judges of the United States courts?
19. Who determine the compensation of the judges?
20. What limitation is there to the power of Congress in this matter?

21. What officers besides judges are connected with the courts of the United States?

22. What are the duties of the attorney-general and of the district attorneys?

23. What are the duties of the marshals?

24. What are the duties of the clerks?

25. What is treason as defined by the Constitution?

26. What is necessary to convict one of treason?

27. What punishment has Congress ordained for treason?

28. What rights has a citizen of New York when he is in the state of Georgia?

29. Suppose a criminal flees from justice to another state, how can he be arrested?

30. By whom may new states be admitted to the Union?

31. Under what conditions may a new state be formed from a portion of one or more states?

32. What is the power of Congress over the territories of the United States?

33. Do the judges of the territorial courts belong to the national judiciary?

34. Can any state lay aside a republican form of government?

35. What is essential to a sovereign state? *Ans.* That it have power to change its form of government whenever it chooses to do so.

36. Suppose a state should attempt to establish a monarchy, what would Congress and the President do?

37. How does it appear that the Constitution requires their interference? — Art. IV. § 4.

38. In what two ways may the Constitution be amended?

39. In what way have all the amendments been made?

40. Show that the Constitution is supreme. — Art. VI. 2.

41. What officers are required to take an oath or affirmation to support the Constitution?

42. Can any religious test be required as a qualification for office?

CHAPTER XXIII.

AMENDMENTS TO THE CONSTITUTION.

1. *When were most of the amendments to the Constitution made?*

Soon after the adoption of the Constitution.

2. *To what were they owing?*

Several of the states proposed to adopt the Constitution on condition that certain amendments be made; but they were led to adopt it unconditionally, and to recommend the amendments desired.

3. *What action was taken in the matter?*

Congress selected the most important articles thus recommended, and proposed them to the legislatures of the states, by whom they were adopted, and thus became parts of the Constitution.

4. *Can Congress establish a state religion?*

"Congress shall make no law respecting an establishment of religion, or prohibiting the free exercise thereof." — Art. I.

5. *Suppose Congress should make a law favoring one religious denomination at the expense of another?*

It would be unconstitutional.

6. *Can Congress abridge freedom of speech or of the press?*

They cannot make any law "abridging the freedom of speech or of the press." — Art. I.

7. *Do laws forbidding slander and libel abridge the freedom of speech or of the press?*

They do not.

8. *Is the right of petition guaranteed by the Constitution?*

It is; for Congress can pass no law interfering with "the right of the people peaceably to assemble, and to petition the government for a redress of grievances." — Art. I.

9. *Is it the duty of Congress to receive all petitions that are respectfully presented?*

It is.

10. *Can the government disarm the people?*

"A well regulated militia being necessary to the security of a free state, the right of the people to keep and bear arms shall not be infringed." — Art. II.

11. *What is said respecting quartering soldiers?*

"No soldier shall, in time of peace, be quartered in any house, without the consent of the owner, nor in time of war, but in a manner to be prescribed by law." — Art. III.

12. *What is the provision against unreasonable searches and seizures?*

"The right of the people to be secure in their persons, houses, papers, and effects against unreasonable searches and seizures shall not be violated." — Art. IV.

13. *What is required in order that a warrant can be issued by a magistrate?*

"No warrants shall issue but upon probable cause, supported by oath or affirmation, and particularly describing the place to be searched, and the person or things to be seized." — Art. IV.

14. *What is required before a man can be tried for a capital or infamous crime?*

"No person shall be held to answer for a capital, or otherwise infamous crime, unless on a presentment or indictment of a grand jury, except in cases arising in the land or naval forces, or in the militia, when in actual service in time of war or public danger." — Art. V.

15. *What is an indictment?*

An accusation, indorsed by the grand jury, certifying that they have found sufficient evidence of guilt to justify the trial of the accused.

16. *Suppose a man has been tried for his life, and acquitted for want of evidence of his guilt, and afterwards overwhelming proof of his guilt is found?*

He cannot be arrested and tried again; for the Constitution says, "Nor shall any person be subject for the same offence to be twice put in jeopardy of life or limb." — Art. V.

17. *Can any one be compelled to bear witness against himself?*

No one "shall be compelled, in any criminal case, to be a witness against himself, nor be deprived of life, liberty, or property, without due process of law." — Art. V.

18. *Can the government take for the public use the property of citizens?*

Not without just compensation; for the Constitution forbids that "private property be taken for public use without just compensation." — Art. V.

19. *What provision is made for the trial of those accused of crime?*

"In all criminal prosecutions, the accused shall enjoy the right to a speedy and public trial, by an impartial jury of the state and district wherein the crime shall have been committed, which district shall have been previously ascertained by law." — Art. VI.

20. *What injustice does this provision guard against?*

It secures the accused against a long imprisonment before being brought to trial, and prevents them from being taken for trial to a part of the country remote from the scene of the alleged crime.

21. *What further provision is made for justice to the accused?*

The Constitution requires that he "be informed of the nature and cause of the accusation; to be confronted with the witnesses against him; to have compulsory process for obtaining witnesses in his favor; and to have the assistance of counsel for his defence." — Art. VI.

22. *Are such safeguards necessary?*

The history of the past shows that men were often condemned to punishment without knowing the crimes with which they were charged, nor the testimony that was brought against them, and without having the means or opportunity of defence.

23. *What is the provision for trial by jury in suits at common law?*

"In suits at common law, where the value in controversy shall exceed twenty dollars, the right of trial by jury shall be preserved; and no fact tried by a jury shall be otherwise reëxamined in any court of the United States than according to the rules of the common law." — Art. VII.

24. *What is the provision in relation to excessive bail and cruel punishments?*

"Excessive bail shall not be required, nor excessive fines imposed, nor cruel nor unusual punishments inflicted." — Art. VIII.

25. *What is the ninth article of amendment?*

"The enumeration in the Constitution of certain rights shall not be construed to deny or disparage others retained by the people."

26. *What is the tenth article?*

"The powers not delegated to the United States by the Constitution, nor prohibited by it to the states, are reserved to the states respectively, or to the people."

27. *Does the word "expressly" occur before "delegated"?*

It does not.

28. *What is the amendment relating to the judicial power?*

"The judicial power of the United States shall not be construed to extend to any suit in law or equity commenced or prosecuted against any one of the United States by citizens of another state, or by citizens or subjects of a foreign state." — Art. XI.

29. *What was the object of this amendment?*

To prevent suits from being brought against a state by citizens of another state.

30. *If a citizen is wronged by a state, how can he obtain justice?*

By the passage by the legislature of the state of a law for his relief.

31. *What is the last amendment to the Constitution?*

"1. Neither slavery nor involuntary servitude, except as a punishment for crime, whereof the party shall have been duly convicted, shall exist within the United States, or any place subject to their jurisdiction.

"2. Congress shall have power to enforce this article by appropriate legislation."

32. *When was the adoption of this amendment officially announced.*

On December 18, 1865.

CHAPTER XXIV.

CONSTITUTIONS OF THE STATES.

1. *What may be said of the constitutions of the several states?*

They are, in the main, similar to the Constitution of the United States, and similar to one another.

2. *How were they made?*

By conventions of delegates chosen in each state for that purpose.

3. *How do they all divide the powers of government?*

Into the legislative, judicial, and executive departments.

4. *Are all the state legislatures composed of two houses?*

They are.

5. *How often do the legislatures meet?*

In most of the states they meet annually; in some biennially.

6. *Where is the executive power in each state vested?*

In a governor.

7. *Are all the governors possessed of equal powers?*

There is a difference in different states.

8. *Are the judicial systems of the several states similar?*

They are similar in many respects, and yet considerable differences exist.

9. *How are the judges appointed?*

In some states they are appointed by the governor and senate, or by the governor and council; in others, they are appointed by the legislature; and in others, they are elected by the people.

10. *What is the tenure of office of the judges?*

In some states it is during good behavior, and in some they are appointed or elected for a year or term of years.

11. *Wherein does the jurisdiction of the state courts differ from that of the national courts?*

The state courts have jurisdiction of cases which arise under the laws of the state.

12. *Are the operations of the national and state courts perfectly distinct?*

Appeals in some cases are made from the state to the national courts, and in regard to some things, the national and state courts have concurrent jurisdiction.

13. *By what inferior officers is a large part of the judicial business of the country transacted?*

By justices of the peace.

14. *To what is this owing?*

To the fact that they have jurisdiction in smaller matters, in regard to which the great majority of cases of litigation take place.

15. *How are they appointed?*

In some states they are appointed by the state governments, and in others they are elected by the people.

16. *What is the advantage of having state governments in addition to the national government?*

The state governments make and execute the laws required by the peculiar interests of each state.

17. *Could not the general government make those laws?*

It would be impossible for Congress to make the great number of laws which are needed for the well-being of all the people in so extensive a country as the United States.

18. *How are the states divided?*

All the states are divided into counties except South Carolina, which is divided into districts, and Louisiana, which is divided into parishes.

19. *Is there a county government in each county?*

There are certain county officers in each county, and there is a county seat, where courts are held and an office kept for recording legal documents.

20. *How are the counties divided?*

In New England, New York, and some other states, they are divided into townships.

21. *What powers do the townships possess?*

The inhabitants meet annually to elect officers for the township, and to make regulations in regard to local matters.

22. *What is a city government?*

A local government possessing certain powers contained in a charter granted by the legistature of the state.

23. *Where are the legislative powers of the government of the city of New York vested?*

They are vested in a board of aldermen and a board of councilmen, which together constitute the common council of the city.

24. *On what subjects may they legislate?*

On those only which are specified in the charter.

25. *Who is the chief executive officer of the city?*

The mayor.

26. *What is necessary in order that an act of the common council may be valid?*

It must pass both boards, and receive the signature of the mayor.

27. *Suppose he vetoes it?*

It may become valid without his signature, if passed by two thirds of both boards.

28. *Are the city governments in our country similar to one another?*

All the large cities of the Union have charter governments similar to that of New York.

QUESTIONS FOR REVIEW.

AMENDMENTS. — STATE GOVERNMENTS.

1. What did some of the states connect with their ratifications of the Constitution?
2. What action was taken by Congress in regard to these recommendations?
3. Can Congress pass a law for the union of church and state?
4. What does the Constitution secure to every citizen as to his religion?
5. Can Congress pass a law punishing a man for speaking and writing against the government?
6. Why not?
7. Suppose a man is guilty of slander or libel?
8. Is Congress under obligation to receive all petitions that are properly presented?
9. How does that appear?
10. Can Congress prohibit citizens from keeping and bearing arms?
11. What is necessary before a man can be tried for an infamous or a capital crime?
12. Suppose a man has been tried for his life and acquitted?
13. What security does the Constitution furnish against a long imprisonment of the accused before he is tried?
14. What other provisions are there for securing justice to the accused?
15. What provisions against excessive bail and cruel punishments?
16. What was the object of the amendment officially announced on December 18, 1865?
17. How were the state constitutions formed?
18. How do they compare with the Constitution of the United States?
19. How do they all divide the powers of government?
20. Of what are the legislatures of all the states composed?

21. What are the executives of the states called?

22. Are the judiciaries of the states similar to that of the United States?

23. What laws are they to interpret?

24. Can they ever decide contrary to the laws of the United States?

25. What is the tenure of office of the judges?

26. Into what are the states divided?

27. What is the advantage of having state governments?

28. Suppose a state pass a law conflicting with a law of the United States?

CHAPTER XXV.

THE ENGLISH CONSTITUTION.

1. *What kind of a government is the English government?*

A limited hereditary monarchy.

2. *Is it a constitutional government?*

It is.

3. *Has it a written or unwritten Constitution?*

It has no written Constitution, like ours, adopted by the vote of the people.

4. *Of what, then, does it consist?*

It consists partly of established usages having the force of law, and partly of written laws.

5. *How are the powers of the government divided?*

They are divided into the legislative, the judicial, and the executive departments.

6. *Where does the legislative power reside?*

In Parliament.

7. *Of what is Parliament composed?*

Of the House of Commons and the House of Lords.

8. *Of what is the House of Commons composed?*

The House of Commons is composed of six hundred and fifty-five members, chosen by the people.

9. *Who may vote for members of the House of Commons?*

Those citizens who occupy, as owner or tenant, any house or other building of the clear yearly value of not less than ten pounds, provided they have paid the poor rates and assessed taxes.

10. *For what length of time are the members chosen?*

For seven years, unless Parliament is sooner dissolved by the King.

11. *Has the King power to dissolve Parliament?*

He can dissolve Parliament whenever he pleases, and order a new election of members of the House of Commons.

12. *How often does Parliament meet?*

It meets annually.

13. *What are the powers of Parliament?*

The power of Parliament to make laws is unlimited, except by the constitutional usages.

14. *What is necessary in order that a bill may become a law?*

It must receive a majority of the votes of both houses of Parliament, and receive the assent of the King.

15. *What compensation do the members of the House of Commons receive?*

They receive no pecuniary compensation, the honor of being a member being deemed sufficient.

16. *At what age may a man become a member of the House of Commons?*
Twenty-one years.

17. *Where must all bills for revenue originate?*
In the House of Commons.

18. *Can the House of Lords alter or amend such a bill?*
They cannot; they must pass or reject it without alteration.

19. *What power does this give the House of Commons?*
They can attach to a revenue bill any provisions they please, and the lords must assent to them, or reject the bill, and thus leave the government without funds.

20. *Can the Senate of the United States alter and amend a bill for revenue?*
They can.

21. *Who presides over the House of Commons?*
The Speaker, who is chosen by the house, but must be approved by the King.

22. *How is the House of Lords composed?*
The House of Lords is composed of the peers of England, sixteen representative peers of Scotland, and twenty-eight representative peers of Ireland, and the archbishops and bishops of the church of England.

23. *Who are the peers of England?*
The nobility of England.

24. *What are the different orders of nobility?*
Dukes, marquises, earls, viscounts, and barons.

25. *Who succeeds to the title and seat of a peer at his death?*

His oldest son or nearest surviving male heir.

26. *Why do not all the peers of Scotland and Ireland have seats in the House of Lords?*

When Scotland and Ireland were united to the British crown, it was agreed that the peers of Scotland should elect sixteen of their number, and the peers of Ireland twenty-eight, to have seats in the House of Lords.

27. *Who is the presiding officer of the House of Lords?*

The Lord High Chancellor.

28. *Where does the power of impeachment reside?*

In the House of Commons.

29. *By whom are impeachments tried?*

By the House of Lords.

30. *What punishment may be inflicted in case of conviction?*

Removal from, and disqualification for, holding office, banishment, forfeiture of goods, imprisonment, and death.

31. *Are the sessions of Parliament open to spectators?*

No one can be present without an order for admission signed by some member.

CHAPTER XXVI.

THE ENGLISH EXECUTIVE.

1. *Where does the executive power reside?*

In the King.

2. *What is a maxim of the English Constitution in regard to the King?*

"The King can do no wrong."

3. *What is the meaning of that maxim?*

The responsibility of all executive acts rests not with the King, but with his ministers.

4. *Who are the ministers?*

Men appointed by the King to conduct the executive affairs of the government.

5. *Are the ministers responsible for all the official acts of the King?*

They are.

6. *Suppose the King commands them to do an illegal act?*

They can be punished for doing it.

7. *How could they avoid doing the illegal act?*

By resigning their offices.

8. *What constitutes the administration in the British government?*

The King's ministers.

9. *What is their tenure of office?*

They hold office at the will of the King.

10. *Can the ministers be also members of the House of Commons?*

They may; but they must be elected after they have been appointed ministers.

11. *What usually takes place when a majority of the House of Commons is opposed to the measures of the administration?*

The ministers resign, and new ministers are appointed, whose views are supposed to correspond with those of the majority of the House of Commons.

12. *What other course is sometimes taken?*

They advise the King to dissolve Parliament, and order the election of a new House of Commons.

13. *When is this course taken?*

When the ministers believe that they can secure in the new house a majority favorable to their views.

14. *What power has the King with respect to war and peace?*

He has the sole power to declare war and make peace.

15. *Does not this give the King nearly absolute power?*

No; for he cannot carry on war without money, and he can get no money unless it is voted by a majority of the House of Commons.

16. *The sword and the purse, then, are not in the same hands?*

The King holds the sword, and the House of Commons the purse.

17. *By whom are all civil and military officers of the government appointed?*

By the King.

18. *What is their tenure of office?*

All officers, except the judges, hold office at the will of the King.

19. *What is the relation of the King to the established church?*

He is the head of the church.

20. *By whom are the bishops appointed?*

By the King acting by his ministers.

21. *Can the King suspend or alter any law?*

He cannot.

22. *Does he possess an absolute veto on all acts of Parliament?*

He does; but that power has not been exercised for nearly two centuries.

23. *What is meant by the maxim, "The King never dies"?*

That the executive department is never vacant. As soon as the King dies, his successor is immediately clothed with all his authority.

24. *Of whom does the Privy Council consist?*

The Privy Council consists of such persons as the King sees fit to appoint.

25. *What power has the Privy Council?*

It has power to decide questions relating to colonial charters and rights, and in relation to commerce.

CHAPTER XXVII.

THE ENGLISH JUDICIARY.

1. *What is the highest court in England?*

The High Court of Chancery.

2. *Who presides over it?*

The Lord High Chancellor.

3. *By whom is he appointed?*
By the King.

4. *What is his tenure of office?*
The will of the King; but as he is a cabinet officer, he usually comes into and goes out of office with the administration.

5. *Is the Court of Chancery solely a court of equity?*
It is both a court of equity and of common law; but the equitable jurisdiction constitutes its principal business.

6. *What inferior Courts of Chancery are there?*
The Court of the Master of the Rolls, and the Courts of the Vice-Chancellors of England.

7. *What are the Superior Courts of Westminster Hall?*
The King's Bench, the Common Pleas, and the Court of Exchequer.

8. *Were the jurisdictions of these courts originally distinct?*
They were.

9. *What cases did the King's Bench take cognizance of?*
Criminal cases.

10. *What suits were brought before the Common Pleas?*
Suits respecting land titles and contracts.

11. *To what did the jurisdiction of the Court of Exchequer relate?*
To matters relating to the King's revenue.

12. *What may be said of the jurisdiction of these courts now?*

The three courts possess concurrent jurisdiction in all civil matters, except that real actions must be brought in the Court of Common Pleas.

13. *What is a real action?*

An action relating to real estate.

14. *Of what does the Court of the King's Bench consist?*

Of one Chief Justice, and four *puisné* judges, as they are termed.

15. *Of what does the Common Pleas consist?*

Of a Chief Justice and four *puisné* judges.

16. *Of what does the Court of Exchequer consist?*

Of one Chief Baron and four *puisné* barons.

17. *How are the judges appointed?*

By the King.

18. *What is their tenure of office?*

During good behavior.

19. *Which court of the three Superior Courts is the highest in rank?*

The King's Bench.

20. *Which is next in rank?*

The Common Pleas.

21. *To what body may appeals from the Court of Chancery and the Courts of Westminster Hall be taken?*

To the House of Lords.

22. *Who always presides when the House of Lords sits as a court of appeal in civil trials?*

The Lord High Chancellor.

23. *What other members of the legal profession are always present?*
The judges of the Superior Courts of Westminster Hall and the attorney-general.

24. *Do they take any part in the proceedings?*
Their opinions are taken on all difficult questions.

25. *What original criminal jurisdiction does the House of Lords possess?*
All peers of the realm are exempt from trial by jury for treason and felony, and can be tried for those crimes only by the House of Lords.

26. *What is the Court of Admiralty?*
A court that takes cognizance of causes relating to maritime affairs.

CHAPTER XXVIII.

INTERNATIONAL LAW.

1. *What is international law?*
The rules that regulate the intercourse of nations.

2. *What should those rules be founded on?*
Justice.

3. *What do they consist of?*
The usages to which all Christian nations have given their assent.

4. *Is international law the result of legislation?*
It is not. There is no international legislature to make laws for the government of the nations.

5. *When does a rule or principle become a part of international law?*

When it has received the assent of all the nations of Christendom.

6. *In the view of international law, what relation do nations sustain to one another?*

The relation of equality.

7. *What follows from this equality?*

That every nation has a right to regulate its own concerns, and that no nation should interfere with the internal affairs of another.

8. *What effect do changes in the government of a nation have on its relations to other nations?*

They have no effect. Treaties formed with a nation under a kingly government remain in force though that kingly government be changed to a democracy.

9. *What does the jurisdiction of a nation embrace?*

A nation has exclusive jurisdiction over all its territory, and over the adjoining sea to the extent of a marine league from the shore.

10. *To whom does the open sea belong?*

The open sea is the common property of all nations.

11. *What rights have foreigners residing in a country?*

They are subject to the laws of the country in which they reside, and can claim protection and justice, though they cannot claim all the privileges of citizens.

12. *Are ambassadors residing in a foreign country subject to its laws?*

They are not. They are the representatives of the country from which they are sent, and are subject to its laws only.

13. *What is a treaty?*

A treaty is a contract between two or more nations.

14. *Suppose one party violates the treaty?*

The other party is released from obligation to observe it.

15. *Suppose a nation is treated unjustly by another, and is refused redress?*

Then war is its only means of redress.

16. *Is a formal declaration of war, and notice thereof to the enemy, necessary before commencing hostilities?*

It is not. After a declaration of war within its own territory, a nation may commence hostilities.

17. *What is the effect of a state of war on commerce?*

A state of war renders all commercial intercourse between the citizens of the nations at war unlawful.

18. *What property is liable to capture?*

An enemy's property of whatever character at sea is liable to capture and confiscation.

19. *What must be done with property thus captured?*

It must be brought into port, and condemned by a prize court sitting in the country of the captor or of an ally, before it can be appropriated by the captor.

20. *May any one capture the enemy's property at sea?*

Those only can make captures who have commissions from the government.

21. *When two or more nations are at war, what is the duty of other nations?*

All other nations are bound to maintain an impartial neutrality.

22. *What are the rights of neutrals?*

Neutral nations have a right to carry on their ordinary commerce with the nations at war. They must not deal in articles contraband of war.

23. *What are contraband articles?*

Arms and ammunition and other articles used in military operations.

24. *From what are neutrals prohibited?*

Neutrals are prohibited from trading with ports that are under blockade.

25. *When is a port blockaded?*

When there is at hand a force sufficient to prevent vessels from leaving or from entering it.

26. *What is the penalty of attempting to violate the blockade?*

The confiscation of the ship and cargo, if captured.

27. *Suppose a neutral is in the port at the time the blockade is declared?*

He is allowed to depart with goods previously purchased.

28. *What is the right of search?*

The right of public armed vessels of the belligerents to visit and search the vessels of neutrals, in order to determine whether property or despatches of the enemy, or contraband goods, are on board.

29. *What is a truce?*

A truce or armistice is a temporary suspension of he operations of war.

30. *What can be done during a truce?*

Nothing to the prejudice of either party by the other which could have been prevented in war.

31. *Is piracy forbidden by the law of nations?*

It is. Piracy is an offence against all nations, and is punishable by all, at will.

32. *Is international law recognized in the legislation of nations?*

It is. Nations have laws rendering its violation penal. According to Blackstone, it is in England held to be a part of the law of the land.

33. *How is it viewed by the United States?*

The United States, by acts of Congress and by judicial decisions, have endeavored to maintain its obligations.

QUESTIONS FOR REVIEW.

CONSTITUTION OF GREAT BRITAIN.

1. What is the government of Great Britain?
2. Has it a written constitution?
3. How are the powers of government divided?
4. Where does the legislative power reside?
5. Of what is Parliament composed?
6. Of what is the House of Commons composed?
7. Of what is the House of Lords composed?
8. How does the mode of passing laws compare with that of Congress?
9. Where must all bills for revenue originate?
10. Can the Lords alter or amend a revenue bill?

11. Can the Senate alter or amend such a bill?
12. Who presides over the House of Commons?
13. Who presides over the House of Lords?
14. What is necessary that one may be admitted to witness the deliberations of each house of Parliament?
15. Are the ordinary sessions of Congress open to all?
16. Where does the power of impeachment reside?
17. Where are impeachments tried?
18. What punishments may follow conviction on impeachment?
19. Wherein does the Constitution of the United States differ in this respect?
20. Where is the executive power vested?
21. What is meant by the maxim, "The King never dies"?
22. How does the King exercise his power?
23. Who are his ministers?
24. Who constitute the administration?
25. What is meant by the maxim, "The King can do no wrong"?
26. Who are responsible for all executive acts?
27. May the ministers be members of Parliament?
28. May the members of the United States cabinet have seats in Congress?
29. Can military officers have seats in Parliament?
30. By whom can Parliament be dissolved?
31. Has the President any such power over Congress?
32. When is Parliament usually dissolved?
33. Who has the sole power to declare war and make peace?
34. Who must furnish the money to carry on war?
35. Who may declare war on the part of the United States?
36. Who may make peace?
37. Who has the control of the public purse of Great Britain?
38. Who appoints all civil and military officers?
39. Who has power to give titles of nobility?
40. Who is the head of the established church?
41. Of whom does the Privy Council consist?
42. What powers have the Privy Council?
43. What is the highest court of England?
44. Who presides in this court?

45. What is his tenure of office?
46. What are the three Courts of Westminster Hall?
47. Which is the highest in rank?
48. Of what does the King's Bench consist?
49. Of what does the Common Pleas consist?
50. Of what does the Court of Exchequer?
51. What is the tenure of office of the judges?
52. What is the final court of appeal for all the higher courts?

CHAPTER XXIX.

DIFFERENT KINDS OF LAW.

1. *What is divine law?*

Divine law is the will of God.

2. *What relation should all laws sustain to it?*

All other laws should be conformed to it.

3. *What is constitutional law?*

A system of fundamental rules determining the form of the government and the extent of its power.

4. *What is international law?*

A system of rules assented to by all the nations of Christendom for the regulation of their intercourse in peace and war.

5. *What is municipal law?*

Municipal law is a rule of civil conduct prescribed by the supreme power in the state. Municipal law is composed of written and unwritten law; that is, statute and common law.

6. *What is statute law?*

Statute law "is the express *written* will of the legislature, rendered authentic by certain prescribed forms and ceremonies."

7. *What is common law?*

"Common law," says Burrill, "is that branch of the law of England which does not owe its origin to parliamentary enactment, being a collection of customs, rules, and maxims which have acquired the force of law by immemorial usage recognized and declared by judicial proceedings."

8. *What is the civil law?*

The civil law is the Roman law, as comprised in the Code, Institutes, Pandects, and Novels of the Emperor JUSTINIAN and his successors.

9. *What is the Code?*

"The Code, in twelve books, is a collection of all the imperial statutes that were thought worth preserving from Hadrian to Justinian."

10. *What are the Institutes?*

"The Institutes, or elements of Roman law, in four books, contain the fundamental principles of the ancient law in a small body, for the use and benefit of students at law."

11. *What are the Pandects?*

The Pandects are an abridgment, in fifty books, of the decisions of prætors and the writings and opinions of the ancient sages in the law.

12. *What are the Novels?*

The Novels of Justiaian are a collection of imperial statutes passed subsequently to the date of the Code, and intended to supply the omissions and correct the errors of the preceding publications.

13. *What influence has the Roman law had on the legislation of modern Europe?*

The Roman law lies at the foundation of all the legislative systems of Europe, except that of England.

14. *What is the canon law?*

The canon law is a collection of ordinances for the regulation of the polity and discipline of the church of Rome.

15. *What is martial law?*

Martial law is a system of rules for the government of an army. When martial law is proclaimed in a city or district, municipal law is suspended, and the will of the military commander becomes the supreme law.

16. *What is parliamentary law?*

It is a system of rules for regulating the proceedings of legislative and other deliberative bodies.

17. *Whence were these rules originally derived?*

They were originally derived from the usages of the British Parliament, and have been, with some modifications, adopted by Congress and the state legislatures.

18. *Are not all deliberative bodies at liberty to make their own rules?*

They are; but the same rules have been very generally adopted by all parliamentary bodies.

QUESTIONS FOR REVIEW.

INTERNATIONAL LAW.—DIFFERENT KINDS OF LAW.

1. What is international law?

2. When does a rule or principle become a part of international law?

3. What relations do nations sustain to one another in the view of international law?

4. May one country interfere with the domestic concerns of other nations?

5. What effect has a change of government in a nation on its relations to other nations?

6. What is the remedy when one nation injures another, and refuses to make redress?

7. What effect has war on the lawfulness of commercial intercourse between the people of the nations at war?

8. What property of an enemy is liable to capture?

9. May any one capture and appropriate the property of an enemy?

10. When war exists between two or more nations, what is the duty of other nations?

11. What rights have neutrals as to trade?

12. What are contraband goods?

13. When is a port blockaded?

14. What is the penalty of violating a blockade?

15. To whom does the sea belong?

16. How far from land does the jurisdiction of a country extend?

17. What is a treaty?

18. Suppose one party fails to observe its stipulations?

19. What is the moral or divine law? *Ans.* The law of right.

20. What is the standard of this law? *Ans.* The will of God.

21. What relation should all other kinds of law sustain to it?

22. What is constitutional law?
23. What is municipal law?
24. What is statute law?
25. What is the common law?
26. What is the civil law?
27. What is the Code?
28. What are the Institutes?
29. What are the Pandects?
30. What are the Novels?
31. What is canon law?
32. What is martial law?
33. What is parliamentary law?

CONSTITUTION

OF THE

UNITED STATES OF AMERICA.

NOTE BY THE PUBLISHERS.—The Constitution and Amendments are here printed with the orthography, punctuation, and capitals of the original documents, as certified to by the Hon. William H. Seward, Secretary of State. The figures, however, at the heads of the parts of the sections are not in the originals: they are here used for convenience in reference.

PREAMBLE.

WE, the People of the United States, in order to form a more perfect Union, establish Justice, insure domestic Tranquillity, provide for the common defence, promote the general Welfare, and secure the Blessings of Liberty to ourselves and our Posterity, do ordain and establish this CONSTITUTION for the United States of America.

ARTICLE I.

SECTION 1.—(1.) All legislative Powers herein granted shall be vested in a Congress of the United States, which shall consist of a Senate and House of Representatives.

SEC. 2.—(1.) The House of Representatives shall be composed of Members chosen every second Year by the People of the several States, and the Electors in each State shall have the Qualifications requisite for Electors of the most numerous Branch of the State Legislature.

(2.) No Person shall be a Representative who shall not have attained to the Age of twenty-five Years, and been seven Years a Citizen of the United States, and who shall not, when elected, be an Inhabitant of that state in which he shall be chosen.

(3.) Representatives and direct Taxes shall be apportioned among the several States which may be included within this Union, according to their respective Numbers, which shall be determined by adding to the whole Number of free Persons, including those bound to Service for a Term of Years, and excluding Indians not taxed, three fifths of all other Persons. The actual Enumeration shall be made within three Years after the first Meeting of the Congress of the United States, and within every subsequent Term of ten Years, in such Manner as they shall by Law direct. The Number of Representatives shall not exceed one for every thirty Thousand, but each State shall have at Least one Representative; and until such enumeration shall be made, the State of New Hampshire shall be entitled to chuse three, Massachusetts eight, Rhode Island and Providence Plantations one, Connecticut five, New York six, New Jersey four, Pennsylvania eight, Delaware one, Maryland six, Virginia ten, North Carolina five, South Carolina five, and Georgia three.

(4.) When vacancies happen in the Representation from any State, the Executive Authority thereof shall issue Writs of Election to fill such Vacancies.

(5.) The House of Representatives shall chuse their Speaker and other Officers; and shall have the sole Power of Impeachment.

SEC. 3.—(1.) The Senate of the United States shall be composed of two Senators from each State, chosen by the Legislature thereof, for six Years; and each Senator shall have one Vote.

(2.) Immediately after they shall be assembled in Consequence of the first Election, they shall be divided as equally as may be into three Classes. The Seats of the Senators of the first Class shall be vacated at the Expiration of the second Year, of the second Class at the Expiration of the fourth Year, and of the third Class at the Expiration of the sixth Year, so that one third may be chosen every second Year; and if Vacancies happen by Resignation, or otherwise, during the Recess of the Legislature of any State, the Executive thereof may make temporary Appointments until the next Meeting of the Legislature, which shall then fill such Vacancies.

(3.) No Person shall be a Senator who shall not have attained to the Age of thirty Years, and been nine Years a Citizen of the United States, and who shall not, when elected, be an Inhabitant of that State for which he shall be chosen.

(4.) The Vice-President of the United States shall be President of the Senate, but shall have no Vote, unless they be equally divided.

(5.) The Senate shall chuse their other Officers, and also a President pro tempore, in the Absence of the Vice-President, or when he shall exercise the Office of President of the United States.

(6.) The Senate shall have the sole Power to try all Impeachments. When sitting for that Purpose, they shall be on Oath or Affirmation. When the President of the United States is tried, the Chief Justice shall preside: And no Person shall be convicted without the Concurrence of two thirds of the Members present.

(7.) Judgment, in Cases of Impeachment shall not extend further than to removal from Office, and Disqualification to hold and enjoy any Office of honour, Trust or Profit under the United States: but the Party convicted shall nevertheless be liable and subject to Indictment, Trial, Judgment and Punishment, according to Law.

SEC. 4.—(1.) The Times, Places and Manner of holding Elections for Senators and Representatives, shall be prescribed in each State by the Legislature thereof; but the Congress may at any time by Law make or alter such Regulations, except as to the places of chusing Senators.

(2.) The Congress shall assemble at least once in every Year, and such Meeting shall be on the first Monday in December, unless they shall by Law appoint a different Day.

SEC. 5.—(1.) Each House shall be the Judge of the Elections, Returns and Qualifications of its own Members, and a Majority of each shall constitute a Quorum to do Business; but a smaller Number may adjourn from day to day, and may be authorized to compel the Attendance of absent Members, in such Manner, and under such Penalties as each House may provide.

(2.) Each House may determine the Rules of its Proceedings, punish its Members for disorderly Behaviour, and, with the Concurrence of two thirds, expel a Member.

(3.) Each House shall keep a Journal of its Proceedings, and from time to time publish the same, excepting such Parts as may in their Judgment require Secrecy; and the Yeas and

Nays of the Members of either House on any question shall, at the Desire of one fifth of those Present, be entered on the Journal.

(4.) Neither House, during the Session of Congress, shall, without the Consent of the other, adjourn for more than three days, nor to any other Place than that in which the two Houses shall be sitting.

SEC. 6.—(1.) The Senators and Representatives shall receive a Compensation for their Services, to be ascertained by Law, and paid out of the Treasury of the United States. They shall in all Cases, except Treason, Felony and Breach of the Peace, be privileged from Arrest during their Attendance at the session of their respective Houses, and in going to and returning from the same; and for any Speech or Debate in either House, they shall not be questioned in any other Place.

(2.) No Senator or Representative shall, during the Time for which he was elected, be appointed to any civil Office under the Authority of the United States, which shall have been created, or the Emoluments whereof shall have been increased during such time; and no Person holding any Office under the United States, shall be a Member of either House during his Continuance in Office.

SEC. 7.—(1.) All Bills for raising Revenue shall originate in the House of Representatives; but the Senate may propose or concur with Amendments as on other Bills.

(2.) Every Bill which shall have passed the House of Representatives and the Senate, shall, before it become a Law, be presented to the President of the United States; If he approve he shall sign it, but if not he shall return it, with his Objections to that House in which it shall have originated, who shall enter the Objections at large on their Journal, and proceed to reconsider it. If after such Reconsideration two thirds of that House shall agree to pass the Bill, it shall be sent, together with the Objections, to the other House, by which it shall likewise be reconsidered, and if approved by two thirds of that House, it shall become a Law. But, in all such Cases, the Votes of both Houses shall be determined by yeas and Nays, and the Names of the Persons voting for and against the Bill shall be entered on the Journal of each House respectively. If any Bill shall not be returned by the President within ten Days (Sundays excepted) after it shall have been presented to him, the Same shall be a law, in like Manner as if he had signed it, unless the Congress by their Adjournment prevent its Return, in which case it shall not be a Law.

(3.) Every Order, Resolution, or Vote, to which the Concurrence of the Senate and House of Representatives may be necessary (except on a question of Adjournment) shall be presented to the President of the United States; and before the Same shall take Effect, shall be approved by him, or being disapproved by him, shall be repassed by two thirds of the Senate and House of Representatives, according to the Rules and Limitations prescribed in the Case of a bill.

SEC. 8.—The Congress shall have Power

(1.) To lay and collect Taxes, Duties, Imposts and Excises, to pay the Debts and provide for the common Defence and general Welfare of the United States; but all Duties, Imposts and Excises shall be uniform throughout the United States;

(2.) To borrow Money on the credit of the United States;

(3.) To regulate Commerce with foreign Nations, and among the several States, and with the Indian Tribes;

(4.) To establish an uniform Rule of Naturalization, and uniform Laws on the subject of Bankruptcies throughout the United States;

(5.) To coin Money, regulate the Value thereof, and of foreign Coin, and fix the Standard of Weights and Measures;

(6.) To provide for the Punishment of counterfeiting the Securities and current Coin of the United States;

(7.) To establish Post Offices and post Roads;

(8.) To promote the progress of Science and useful Arts, by securing for limited Times to Authors and Inventors the exclusive Right to their respective Writings and Discoveries;

(9.) To constitute Tribunals inferior to the supreme Court;

(10.) To define and punish Piracies and Felonies committed on the high Seas, and Offences against the Law of Nations;

(11.) To declare War, grant Letters of Marque and Reprisal, and make Rules concerning Captures on Land and Water;

(12.) To raise and support Armies, but no Appropriation of Money to that Use shall be for a longer Term than two Years;

(13.) To provide and maintain a Navy;

(14.) To make Rules for the Government and Regulation of the land and naval Forces;

(15.) To provide for calling forth the Militia to execute the Laws of the Union, suppress Insurrections and repel Invasions;

(16.) To provide for organizing, arming, and disciplining, the Militia, and for governing such Part of them as may be employed in the Service of the United States, reserving to the States respectively, the Appointment of the Officers, and the authority of training the Militia according to the Discipline prescribed by Congress;

(17.) To exercise exclusive Legislation in all Cases whatsoever, over such District (not exceeding ten Miles square) as may, by Cession of particular States, and the Acceptance of Congress, become the Seat of Government of the United States, and to exercise like Authority over all Places purchased by the Consent of the Legislature of the State in which the same shall be, for the Erection of Forts, Magazines, Arsenals, Dock-Yards, and other needful Buildings;—And

(18.) To make all Laws which shall be necessary and proper for carrying into execution the foregoing Powers, and all other powers vested by this Constitution in the Government of the United States, or in any Department or Officer thereof.

SEC. 9.—(1.) The Migration or Importation of such Persons as any of the States now existing shall think proper to admit, shall not be prohibited by the Congress prior to the Year one thousand eight hundred and eight, but a Tax or Duty may be imposed on such Importation, not exceeding ten dollars for each Person.

(2.) The Privilege of the Writ of Habeas Corpus shall not be suspended, unless when in Cases of Rebellion or Invasion the public Safety may require it.

(3.) No Bill of Attainder or ex post facto Law shall be passed.

(4.) No Capitation, or other direct, Tax shall be laid, unless in Proportion to the Census or Enumeration hereinbefore directed to be taken.

(5.) No Tax or Duty shall be laid on Articles exported from any State.

(6.) No Preference shall be given by any Regulation of Commerce or Revenue to the Ports of one State over those of another: nor shall Vessels bound to, or from, one State, be obliged to enter, clear, or pay Duties in another.

(7.) No Money shall be drawn from the Treasury, but in

Consequence of Appropriations made by Law; and a regular Statement and Account of the Receipts and Expenditures of all public Money shall be published from time to time.

(8.) No Title of Nobility shall be granted by the United States: And no Person holding any Office of Profit or Trust under them, shall, without the Consent of the Congress, accept of any present, Emolument, Office, or Title of any kind whatever, from any King, Prince, or foreign State.

SEC. 10.—(1.) No State shall enter into any Treaty, Alliance, or Confederation; grant Letters of Marque and Reprisal; coin Money; emit Bills of Credit; make any Thing but gold and silver Coin a Tender in Payment of Debts; pass any Bill of Attainder, ex post facto Law, or Law impairing the Obligation of Contracts; or grant any Title of Nobility.

(2.) No State shall, without the consent of the Congress, lay any Imposts or Duties on Imports or Exports, except what may be absolutely necessary for executing its inspection Laws: and the net Produce of all Duties and Imposts, laid by any State on Imports or Exports, shall be for the Use of the Treasury of the United States; and all such Laws shall be subject to the Revision and Controul of the Congress.

(3.) No State shall, without the Consent of Congress, lay any Duty of Tonnage, keep Troops, or Ships of War in time of Peace, enter into any Agreement or Compact with another State, or with a foreign Power, or engage in War, unless actually invaded, or in such imminent Danger as will not admit of Delay.

ARTICLE II.

SECTION 1.—(1.) The executive Power shall be vested in a President of the United States of America. He shall hold his Office during the Term of four Years, and, together with the Vice-President, chosen for the same Term, be elected as follows

(2.) Each State shall appoint, in such Manner as the Legislature thereof may direct, a Number of Electors, equal to the whole Number of Senators and Representatives to which the State may be entitled in the Congress: but no Senator or Representative, or Person holding an Office of Trust or Profit under the United States, shall be appointed an Elector.

[3. *The Electors shall meet in their respective States, and vote by Ballot for two Persons, of whom one at least shall not be an Inhabitant of the same State with themselves. And they shall make a List of all the Persons voted for, and of the Number of Votes for each; which List they shall sign and certify, and transmit sealed to the Seat of the Government of the United States, directed to the President of the Senate. The President of the Senate shall, in the Presence of the Senate and House of Representatives, open all the Certificates, and the Votes shall then be counted. The Person having the greatest Number of Votes shall be the President, if such Number be a Majority of the whole Number of Electors appointed; and if there be more than one who have such Majority, and have an equal Number of Votes, then the House of Representatives shall immediately chuse, by Ballot, one of them for President; and if no Person have a Majority, then, from the five highest on the List, the said House shall, in like Manner, chuse the President. But, in chusing the President, the Votes shall be taken by States, the Representation from each State having one Vote; A Quorum for this Purpose shall consist of a Member or Members from two thirds of the States, and a Majority of all the States shall be necessary to a Choice. In every Case, after the Choice of the President, the Person having the greatest Number of Votes of the Electors shall be the Vice-President. But if there should remain two or more who have equal Votes, the Senate shall chuse from them, by Ballot, the Vice-President.]

(4.) The Congress may determine the Time of chusing the Electors, and the Day on which they shall give their Votes; which Day shall be the same throughout the United States.

(5.) No Person except a natural born Citizen, or a Citizen of the United States, at the time of the Adoption of this Constitution, shall be eligible to the Office of President; neither shall any Person be eligible to that Office who shall not have attained to the Age of thirty five Years, and been fourteen Years a Resident within the United States.

(6.) In Case of the Removal of the President from Office, or of his Death, Resignation, or Inability to discharge the Powers and Duties of the said Office, the same shall devolve on the Vice-President, and the Congress may by Law provide for the Case of Removal, Death, Resignation, or Inability, both of the President and Vice-President, declaring what Officer shall then act as President, and such Officer shall act accordingly, until the Disability be removed, or a President shall be elected.

(7.) The President shall, at stated Times, receive for his Services, a Compensation, which shall neither be encreased nor diminished during the Period for which he shall have been elected, and he shall not receive within that Period any other Emolument from the United States, or any of them.

---

* This has been changed by Article XII. of the Amendments. See page 133.

(8.) Before he enter on the Execution of his Office, he shall take the following Oath or Affirmation:—

"I do solemnly swear (or affirm) that I will faithfully execute the Office of President of the United States, and will to the best of my Ability, preserve, protect, and defend the Constitution of the United States."

SEC. 2.—(1.) The President shall be Commander in Chief of the Army and Navy of the United States, and of the Militia of the several States, when called into the actual Service of the United States; he may require the Opinion, in writing, of the principal Officer in each of the executive Departments, upon any Subject relating to the Duties of their respective Offices, and he shall have Power to grant Reprieves and Pardons for Offences against the United States, except in Cases of Impeachment.

(2.) He shall have Power, by and with the Advice and Consent of the Senate, to make Treaties, provided two thirds of the Senators present concur; and he shall nominate, and by and with the Advice and Consent of the Senate, shall appoint, Ambassadors, other public Ministers and Consuls, Judges of the supreme Court, and all other Officers of the United States, whose Appointments are not herein otherwise provided for, and which shall be established by Law: but the Congress may by Law vest the Appointment of such inferior Officers, as they think proper, in the President alone, in the Courts of Law, or in the Heads of Departments.

(3.) The President shall have Power to fill up all Vacancies that may happen during the Recess of the Senate, by granting Commissions which shall expire at the end of their next Session.

SEC. 3.—(1.) He shall from time to time give to the Congress Information of the State of the Union, and recommend to their Consideration such Measures as he shall judge necessary and expedient. He may, on extraordinary Occasions, convene both Houses, or either of them, and in Case of Disagreement between them, with Respect to the Time of Adjournment, he may adjourn them to such Time as he shall think proper: he shall receive Ambassadors and other public Ministers: he shall take Care that the Laws be faithfully executed; and shall Commission all the officers of the United States.

SEC. 4.—(1.) The President, Vice President, and all civil Officers of the United States, shall be removed from Office on

Impeachment for, and Conviction of, Treason, Bribery, or other high Crimes and Misdemeanors.

ARTICLE III.

SECTION 1.—(1.) The judicial Power of the United States, shall be vested in one supreme Court, and in such inferior Courts as the Congress may from time to time ordain and establish. The Judges, both of the supreme and inferior Courts, shall hold their Offices during good Behaviour, and shall, at stated Times, receive for their Services, a Compensation which shall not be diminished during their Continuance in Office.

SEC. 2.—(1.) The judicial Power shall extend to all Cases, in Law and Equity, arising under this Constitution, the Laws of the United States, and Treaties made, or which shall be made, under their Authority;—to all Cases affecting Ambassadors, other public Ministers, and Consuls;—to all Cases of admiralty and maritime Jurisdiction;—to Controversies to which the United States shall be a Party;—to Controversies between two or more States;—between a State and Citizens of another State;—between Citizens of different States;—between Citizens of the same State claiming Lands under Grants of different States, and between a State, or the Citizens thereof, and foreign States, Citizens or Subjects.

(2.) In all Cases affecting Ambassadors, other public Ministers and Consuls, and those in which a State shall be Party, the supreme Court shall have original Jurisdiction. In all the other Cases before mentioned, the supreme Court shall have appellate Jurisdiction, both as to Law and Fact, with such Exceptions, and under such Regulations as the Congress shall make.

(3.) The Trial of all Crimes, except in Cases of Impeachment, shall be by Jury; and such Trial shall be held in the State where the said Crimes shall have been committed; but when not committed within any State, the Trial shall be at such Place or Places as the Congress may by Law have directed.

SEC. 3.—(1.) Treason against the United States, shall consist only in levying War against them, or in adhering to their Enemies, giving them Aid and Comfort. No Person shall be convicted of Treason unless on the Testimony of two Witnesses to the same overt Act, or on Confession in open Court.

(2.) The Congress shall have Power to declare the Punishment of Treason, but no Attainder of Treason shall work Corruption of Blood, or Forfeiture except during the Life of the Person attainted.

ARTICLE IV.

SECTION 1.—(1.) Full Faith and Credit shall be given in each State to the public Acts, Records, and judicial Proceedings of every other State. And the Congress may by general Laws prescribe the Manner in which such Acts, Records and Proceedings shall be proved, and the Effect thereof.

SEC. 2.—(1.) The Citizens of each State shall be entitled to all Privileges and Immunities of Citizens in the several States.

(2.) A Person charged in any State with Treason, Felony, or other Crime, who shall flee from Justice, and be found in another State, shall on Demand of the executive Authority of the State from which he fled, be delivered up, to be removed to the State having Jurisdiction of the Crime.

(3.) No Person held to Service or Labour in one State, under the Laws thereof, escaping into another, shall, in Consequence of any Law or Regulation therein, be discharged from such Service or Labour, but shall be delivered up on Claim of the Party to whom such Service or Labour may be due.

SEC. 3.—(1.) New States may be admitted by the Congress into this Union ; but no new State shall be formed or erected within the Jurisdiction of any other State ; nor any State be formed by the Junction of two or more States, or Parts of States, without the Consent of the Legislatures of the States concerned, as well as of the Congress.

(2.) The Congress shall have Power to dispose of, and make all needful Rules and Regulations respecting the Territory or other Property belonging to the United States ; and nothing in this Constitution shall be so construed as to Prejudice any Claims of the United States, or of any particular State.

SEC. 4.—(1.) The United States shall guarantee to every State in this Union a Republican Form of Government, and shall protect each of them against Invasion, and, on Application of the Legislature, or of the Executive (when the Legislature cannot be convened) against domestic Violence.

ARTICLE V.

(1.) The Congress, whenever two thirds of both Houses shall deem it necessary, shall propose Amendments to this Constitution, or, on the Application of the Legislatures of two thirds of the several States, shall call a Convention for proposing Amendments, which, in either Case, shall be valid to all Intents and Purposes, as Part of this Constitution, when ratified by the Legislatures of three fourths of the several States, or by Conventions in three fourths thereof, as the one or the other Mode of Ratification may be proposed by the Congress; Provided that no Amendment which may be made prior to the Year one thousand eight hundred and eight shall in any Manner affect the first and fourth Clauses in the Ninth Section of the first Article; and that no State, without its Consent, shall be deprived of its equal Suffrage in the Senate.

ARTICLE VI.

(1.) All Debts contracted and Engagements entered into, before the Adoption of this Constitution, shall be as valid against the United States under this Constitution, as under the Confederation.

(2.) This Constitution, and the Laws of the United States which shall be made in Pursuance thereof; and all Treaties made, or which shall be made, under the authority of the United States, shall be the supreme Law of the Land; and the Judges in every State shall be bound thereby, any Thing in the Constitution or Laws of any State to the Contrary notwithstanding.

(3.) The Senators and Representatives before mentioned, and the Members of the several State Legislatures, and all executive and Judicial Officers, both of the United States and of the several States, shall be bound by Oath or Affirmation, to support this Constitution; but no religious Test shall ever be required as a Qualification to any Office or public Trust under the United States.

ARTICLE VII.

(1.) The Ratification of the Conventions of nine States, shall be sufficient for the Establishment of this Constitution between the States so ratifying the Same.

Done in Convention by the Unanimous Consent of the States present the Seventeenth Day of September in the Year of our Lord one thousand seven hundred and Eighty seven and of the Independance of the United States of America the Twelfth IN WITNESS whereof We have hereunto subscribed our Names,

GEO WASHINGTON —
Presidt and deputy from Virginia.

NEW HAMPSHIRE.

John Langdon,
Nicholas Gilman.

MASSACHUSETTS.

Nathaniel Gorham,
Rufus King.

CONNECTICUT.

Wm. Saml. Johnson,
Roger Sherman.

NEW YORK.

Alexander Hamilton.

NEW JERSEY.

Wil: Livingston,
David Brearley,
Wm. Paterson,
Jona. Dayton.

PENNSYLVANIA.

B. Franklin,
Robt. Morris,
Tho: Fitzsimons,
James Wilson,
Thomas Mifflin,
Geo: Clymer,
Jared Ingersoll,
Gouv: Morris.

DELAWARE.

Geo: Read,
John Dickinson,
Jaco: Broom,
Gunning Bedford, Jun'r.,
Richard Bassett,

MARYLAND.

James M'Henry
Danl. Carroll,
Dan: of St. Thos. Jenifer.

VIRGINIA.

John Blair,
James Madison, Jr.,

NORTH CAROLINA.

Wm. Blount,
Hu. Williamson.
Rich'd Dobbs Spaight.

SOUTH CAROLINA.

J. Rutledge,
Charles Pinckney,
Charles Cotesworth Pinckney,
Pierce Butler.

GEORGIA.

William Few,
Abr. Baldwin.

ATTEST:

WILLIAM JACKSON, *Secretary.*

ARTICLES IN ADDITION TO, AND AMENDMENTS OF THE CONSTITUTION.

PROPOSED BY CONGRESS, AND RATIFIED BY THE LEGISLATURES OF THE SEVERAL STATES, PURSUANT TO THE FIFTH ARTICLE OF THE ORIGINAL CONSTITUTION.

ARTICLE I. Congress shall make no law respecting an establishment of religion, or prohibiting the free exercise thereof; or abridging the freedom of speech, or of the press; or the right of the people peaceably to assemble, and to petition the Government for a redress of grievances.

ART. II. A well-regulated Militia, being necessary to the security of a free State, the right of the people to keep and bear Arms, shall not be infringed.

ART. III. No Soldier shall, in time of peace be quartered in any house, without the consent of the Owner, nor in time of war, but in a manner to be prescribed by law.

ART. IV. The right of the people to be secure in their persons, houses, papers, and effects, against unreasonable searches and seizures, shall not be violated, and no Warrants shall issue, but upon probable cause, supported by Oath or affirmation, and particularly describing the place to be searched, and the persons or things to be seized.

ART. V. No person shall be held to answer for a capital, or otherwise infamous crime, unless on a presentment or indictment of a Grand Jury, except in cases arising in the land or naval forces, or in the Militia, when in actual service in time of War or public danger; nor shall any person be subject for the same offence to be twice put in jeopardy of life or limb; nor shall be compelled in any Criminal Case to be a witness against himself, nor be deprived of life, liberty, or property, without due process of law; nor shall private property be taken for public use, without just compensation.

ART. VI. In all criminal prosecutions, the accused shall enjoy the right to a speedy and public trial, by an impartial jury of the State and district wherein the crime shall have been committed, which district shall have been previously ascertained by law, and to be informed of the nature and cause of the accusation; to be confronted with the witnesses against him; to have Compulsory process for obtaining Witnesses in his favor and to have the Assistance of Counsel for his defence.

ART. VII. In Suits at common law, where the value in controversy shall exceed twenty dollars, the right of trial by jury shall be preserved, and no fact tried by a jury shall be otherwise re-examined in any Court of the United States, than according to the rules of the common law.

ART. VIII. Excessive bail shall not be required, nor excessive fines imposed, nor cruel and unusual punishments inflicted.

ART. IX. The enumeration in the Constitution of certain rights, shall not be construed to deny or disparage others retained by the people.

ART. X. The powers not delegated to the United States by the Constitution, nor prohibited by it to the States, are reserved to the States respectively, or to the people.

ART. XI. The Judicial power of the United States shall not be construed to extend to any suit in law or equity commenced or prosecuted against one of the United States by Citizens of another State, or by Citizens or Subjects of any Foreign State.

ART. XII. The Electors shall meet in their respective states, and vote by ballot for President and Vice-President, one of whom, at least, shall not be an inhabitant of the same state with themselves; they shall name in their ballots the person voted for as President, and in distinct ballots the person voted for as Vice-President, and they shall make distinct lists of all persons voted for as President, and of all persons voted for as Vice-President, and of the number of votes for each, which lists they shall sign and certify, and transmit sealed to the seat of the government of the United States, directed to the President of the Senate;—the President of the Senate shall, in the presence of the Senate and House of Representatives, open all the certificates and the votes shall then be counted;—the person having the greatest number of votes for President, shall be the President, if such number be a majority of the whole number of Electors appointed; and if no person have such majority, then from the persons having the highest numbers not exceeding three on the list of those voted for as President, the House of Representatives shall choose immediately, by ballot, the President. But, in choosing the President, the votes shall be taken by states, the representation from each state having one vote; a quorum for this purpose shall consist of a member or members from two thirds of the states, and a majority of all the states shall be necessary to a choice. And if the House of Representatives shall not choose a President whenever the right of choice shall devolve upon them, before the fourth day of March next following, then the Vice-President shall act as President, as in the case of the death or other constitutional disability of the President. The person having the greatest number of votes as Vice-President, shall be the Vice-President, if such number be a majority of the whole number of Electors appointed, and if no person have a majority, then from the two highest numbers on the list, the Senate shall choose the Vice-President; a quorum for the purpose shall consist of two thirds of the whole number of Senators, and a majority of the whole number shall be necessary to a choice. But no person constitutionally ineligible to the office of President shall be eligible to that of Vice-President of the United States.

ART. XIII.—SEC. I. Neither slavery nor involuntary servitude, except as a punishment for crime whereof the party shall have been duly convicted, shall exist within the United States, or any place subject to their jurisdiction.

SEC. 2. Congress shall have power to enforce this article by appropriate legislation.

ART. XIV.—SEC. 1. All persons born or naturalized in the United States, and subject to the jurisdiction thereof, are citizens of the United States, and of the State wherein they reside. No State shall make or enforce any law which shall abridge the privileges or immunities of citizens of the United States; nor shall any State deprive any person of life, liberty, or property, without due process of law, nor deny to any person within its jurisdiction the equal protection of the laws.

SEC. 2. Representatives shall be apportioned among the several States according to their respective numbers, counting the whole number of persons in each State, excluding Indians not taxed. But when the right to vote at any election for the choice of Electors for President of the United States, Representatives in Congress, the executive and judicial officers of a State, or the members of the Legislature thereof, is denied to any of the male inhabitants of such State, being twenty-one years of age and citizens of the United States, or in any way abridged, except for participation in rebellion or other crime, the basis of representation therein shall be reduced in the proportion which the number of such male citizens shall bear to the whole number of male citizens twenty-one years of age in such State.

SEC. 3. No person shall be a Senator or Representative in Congress, or Elector of President and Vice-President, or hold any office, civil or military, under the United States, or under any State, who, having previously taken an oath, as a member of Congress, or as a member of any State Legislature, or as an executive or judicial officer of any State, to support the Constitution of the United States, shall have engaged in insurrection or rebellion against the same, or given aid and comfort to the enemies thereof. But Congress may, by a vote of two-thirds of each House, remove such disability.

SEC. 4. The validity of the public debt of the United States, authorized by law, including debts incurred for payment of pensions and bounties for services in suppressing insurrection and rebellion, shall not be questioned. But neither the United States nor any State shall assume or pay any debt or obligation incurred in aid of insurrection or rebellion against the United States, or any claim for the loss or emancipation of any slave; but all such debts, obligations, or claims, shall be held illegal and void.

SEC. 5. Congress shall have power to enforce, by appropriate legislation, the provisions of this article.

ART. XV.—SEC. 1. The right of the citizens of the United States to vote shall not be denied or abridged by the United States, or by any State, on account of race, color, or previous condition of servitude.

SEC. 2. The Congress shall have power to enforce this article by appropriate legislation.

NOTE.—Article XV. was proposed by Congress in 1869, as an amendment to the Constitution, and was declared adopted in March, 1870.

J. H. Porit.

www.ingramcontent.com/pod-product-compliance
Lightning Source LLC
LaVergne TN
LVHW021415110826
845150LV00007B/1936

* 9 7 8 1 4 2 5 5 0 9 7 4 3 *